The Nurse
as Group Leader

CAROLYN CHAMBERS CLARK is a mental health specialist and educator. Currently, she teaches group dynamics and leadership at Pace University—Westchester Graduate School of Nursing and conducts workshops on mental health concepts for nurses at several other major universities. She is also a private practioner in individual, group, and family therapy, as well as a consultant/therapist with two visiting nurse services in Bergen County, New Jersey.

Dr. Clark (Ed.D., Teachers College, Columbia University) is a prolific contributor to professional literature, especially in the areas of psychiatric nursing, group processes, and the use of simulation gaming to teach nursing concepts. *The Nurse as Group Leader* is her second book.

The Nurse
as Group Leader

CAROLYN CHAMBERS CLARK

R.N., Ed.D.

SPRINGER PUBLISHING COMPANY

New York

Springer Publishing Company, Inc.
200 Park Avenue South
New York, N.Y. 10003

77 78 79 80 81 / 10 9 8 7 6 5 4 3 2 1

Library of Congress Cataloging in Publication Data

Clark, Carolyn Chambers.
      The nurse as group leader.

      Includes bibliographies and index.
      1. Nursing service administration. 2. Leaderships.
3. Small groups. I. Title.
RT89.C56   658.3'14   77-7778
ISBN 0-8261-2330-9
ISBN 0-8261-2331-7 pbk.

Printed in the United States of America

For my parents,
Phyllis and John Stark

CONTENTS

ACKNOWLEDGMENTS

I wish to thank the students in the graduate program in Nursing at Pace University—Westchester who shared in the development of the course, Group Dynamics, upon which this book is based.

I also wish to acknowledge the encouragement and support provided by my husband, William F. Clark.

Lastly, I thank Mrs. Helen Behnke for her support and editorial skill.

C.C.C.

PREFACE

I decided to write this book when I was unable to locate a suitable text to use in a basic course in group dynamics. There were many texts on group psychotherapy and some books in the behavioral science areas that covered certain aspects of group skills and theory, but none were broad enough to cover the wide range of group situations within which nurses work; nor did they deal with the specifics of how actually to lead a group. Since the groups with which nurses become involved encompass nursing care planning groups, patient teaching groups, supportive groups for dying patients and their families, patient advocacy groups, and health team planning groups, it is essential that all nurses possess a knowledge of group processes and be proficient in assessment and intervention skills.

The Nurse as Group Leader is meant to fill the gap in nursing education texts by providing nurses with knowledge of how groups work and how to intervene to promote group movement. The word "leader" is used throughout the book to refer both to the nurse who is the formal or designated leader of the group and to the nurse who, while participating in a group, practices effective group skills to exert informal leadership of it.

Because the students I worked with seemed to learn both from group process recordings (with subsequent instructor feedback) and from simulated group experiences, I have given these two learning experiences equal treatment, with theory presentations in the text. Simulated exercises can be found at the end of each chapter, and sample recordings with instructor feedback are presented in Chapter 7.

This book is meant to be used by nursing students and graduate nurses in a variety of settings. It is my hope that upper-level basic nursing students, graduate students, and graduate nurses who work with groups will find the content useful in their efforts to improve their group skills. The book provides a general approach to the concepts of group work and its processes and thus is not designed for nurses majoring in mental health counseling, although it could be used as a supplemental text. It should be remembered also that this text is meant to be used by learners who already have the basic skills of interviewing and communicating in the one-to-one nurse-patient relationship.

Although the pronoun "she" is used throughout the text, the book is directed toward both male and female learners.

Carolyn Chambers Clark

The Nurse
as Group Leader

1

Introduction to Group Work

GROUPS ARE IMPORTANT

Groups are important to people from the moment they are born until their lives end. Socialization first takes place in the group called the family. Later, peer groups, social groups, religious groups, work groups, and political groups become important vehicles for learning and obtaining satisfaction.

The quality of peoples' lives often depends on their ability to perform effectively in the groups to which they belong. The nurse, as a social being, also belongs to many groups. The effectiveness of the nurse in these groups depends on her ability to assess and intervene in the ebb and flow of processes that affect the internal workings of each group.

Group skills are important in nursing for at least two reasons. First, many tasks, such as planning for patient care, cannot be accomplished without the cooperation and collaboration of other health care givers. Nurses, therefore, need to learn to work effectively with their colleagues and with other health care

personnel. Group skills in this kind of cooperation and collaboration are especially important now that nurses are striving to be
recognized as peers by physicians, psychologists, social workers,
and other health care professionals. Since the majority of nurses
are women, the nursing profession is also faced with the necessity
of working through nurse/doctor relationships; since most doctors
are men, this involves working through male/female relationships.
Effective group skills can assist nurses to be clear and assertive
when working with various groups of health care personnel
without resorting to aggressive or helpless behavior, withdrawal,
or apathy.

Second, nursing functions include teaching and supportive
assistance to patients or clients and their families—two functions
that can often best be provided within a group format. Such a
format affords a number of experiences that the one-to-one nurse/
patient relationship cannot provide. Group experiences can also
supply a more intense and different type of support; assistance
in observing a wide range of responses; positive and negative
feedback in a supportive way; pooling of resources and solutions
to problems; knowledge that others share the same difficulty,
fear, or anxiety; validation of one's own perceptions; and more
efficient use of nursing time.

Group skills, then, are important to nurses not only when
they form and lead groups such as clients or families but also
when they are members of a planning or task group. In the latter
case, the nurse may or may not be the designated leader; if she
is not, she can learn to provide informal leadership and thus help
the group to function more effectively.

TYPES OF GROUPS

Nurses work primarily in three types of groups: task groups,
teaching groups, and supportive or therapeutic groups. Figure 1
lists the types of groups with which nurses most often work,
their primary purposes, and examples of groups belonging to
each type.

Figure 1

Types of Groups Amenable to Nurse Leadership

Group Type	Primary Purpose	Examples
Task	Accomplishing the task	Curriculum committee meeting Nursing service planning committee Nursing team meeting Nursing care conference Hospital staff meeting
Teaching	Imparting information	Group continuing education Nutrition group for clients Sex education group for adolescents Sensory-motor group for preschoolers Reality orientation group for nursing home residents
Supportive/ Therapeutic	Dealing with emotional stress	Group for infertile spouses Group for expectant spouses Group for middle-aged people in mid-career crisis Group for people with chronic illness processes Group for rape victims

Task Groups

The primary purpose of task groups is to accomplish a given task; they place high priority on decision making and problem solving. Health care planning committees, nursing service committees, nursing teams, and nursing care conference groups are all examples of task groups in which nurses may participate.

Task groups are often formed to solve a given problem; for example, How can the consumer have input into health care planning? What is the most effective way for the nursing service to function? How can nursing personnel best provide nursing care for a group of 25 patients? How can the nursing staff deal more constructively with Mr. A's behavior?

Task groups are usually under pressure to complete the task within an allotted time period. There is also a tendency to ignore, deny, or try to smooth over any existing conflict.

Teaching Groups

The primary purpose of teaching groups is to impart information to the participants. Although the tendency to separate the learner from the teacher always exists in these groups, at least one research study has shown that students learn as much—or more—when teaching as their peers do (Clark, 1976).

Nurses may participate in a number of teaching/learning groups. Hospitals, institutions, and agencies often present continuing education courses to teach nurses new skills or to enhance previously learned basic skills; in many of these programs, nurses participate with a group of other nurses. A nurse may, on the other hand, utilize the group format in a program designed to teach patients about health care.

When the nurse leads a group in which the primary purpose is to teach or to learn, the following questions need to be considered: Which material is best suited to group or individual learning? Are the students ready to learn? What do they already know? Do the members of the group have similar levels of knowledge? How much repetition of material is needed to enhance learning? How can students be helped to plan and evaluate their own learning experiences? Is the pace of instruction too fast or too slow? How can the teacher provide the students with adequate feedback about how well they are learning the material? How can effective learning behaviors be increased?

Innumerable subjects are suitable for handling via the group-teaching format: labor and childbirth techniques; birth control methods; nutrition; the management of diabetes; the management of colostomies or ileostomies; effective parenting; orientation to nursing-home living; appropriate exercises for nursing-home residents; sensory-motor skills for preschoolers; preparation of families to enable them to care for discharged patients.

Supportive or Therapeutic Groups

The primary purpose of supportive or therapeutic groups is to assist members in dealing with emotional stresses due to hospitalization, illness processes, growth and development crises, situational crises, or socially maladaptive behavior. Supportive or therapeutic groups focus on the examination of members' thoughts, feelings, and subsequent behavior. Patients or clients often benefit from ventilating their feelings, from seeing that others share and accept these feelings, and from learning healthy and constructive ways of coping with them. Supportive or therapeutic groups should not be thought of as a form of group psychotherapy or of psychoanalysis; rather, their concern is to prevent possible future upsets by educating the participants in effective ways of dealing with emotional stress arising from situational or developmental crises.

Supportive or therapeutic groups are usually under less pressure than the teaching and task groups to complete the task during one or two meetings. Another difference is that conflict among the group members may be pursued and explored because it is often related to the ways in which members deal with emotional stress. The leader may even choose to maintain anxiety and conflict at fairly high levels if this serves to assist the group to continue focusing on their feelings, rather than to cover over or withdraw from the discomfort. New tasks, such as how to deal with the entrance of a tardy or new group member, may be generated spontaneously and dealt with by the group.

In convening a supportive or therapeutic group, the nurse frequently gathers together people who are undergoing similar emotional stresses. Such groups may, for example, consist of the families of dying patients; patients with a chronic illness and/or their families; patients who have recently lost a body part through surgery or accident; severely burned patients; pre- or postoperative patients; patients awaiting diagnosis, admission, or hospital discharge; involuntary nursing-home patients; rape

victims; parents of infants with birth defects; clients with a drug
or alcohol problem; prison inmates; patients who have suicidal or
homicidal tendencies; middle-aged men or women facing a career
or mid-career crisis; anxious preschoolers who fear going to school;
child-abusing parents; adolescents with inadequate knowledge
of their current physiological changes and the ramifications; and
identified or potential juvenile delinquents.

CONCERNS OF ALL GROUP LEADERS

Although at first glance it would seem that each group would
demand different group skills, actually, to be effective, all three
types of groups require that a balance be maintained between
adhering to the task and meeting the interpersonal needs of group
members. For example, if the task group leader is so concerned
about following the agenda that she fails to note how upset the
curriculum committee is about a proposed cut in faculty salaries,
the group will not function effectively. Likewise, if the leader in
a teaching group is so concerned about giving information that
she forgets to find out whether all members understand the
information, or if she supports dependency on the leader by
always giving the correct answer herself, group functioning will
not be as effective as it should be. Even in supportive or therapeutic groups, the leader has to maintain a balance between
giving support and working toward a task; since the task may be
to understand one's thoughts and feelings and to learn effective
ways of dealing with them, the leader cannot be too supportive
as this may prevent group members from learning new ways of
coping with their thoughts and feelings. Thus, in all three types
of groups, the nurse-leader is concerned with achieving a balance
between interpersonal and task functions.

QUALITIES OF AN EFFECTIVE GROUP LEADER

A group leader must have a high tolerance for anxiety, frustration, and disorganization. She must be capable of accepting group confrontation, hostility, and conflict without directly or indirectly punishing group members or ignoring the fact that such processes are occurring.

A group leader needs to be able to accept and organize a great deal of information and be capable of observing both verbal and nonverbal messages and making sense out of both. Group interactions can be intense and quick-moving, and the amount of input can overwhelm the novice group leader. With practice and supervision by a skilled group leader, nurses can learn how to organize extensive amounts of information and when and how to intervene in group interaction. At times, the nurse leader must be able to stop listening to what is being said in the group and instead "tune in" on the nonverbal communication that is being conveyed.

Group leaders have to engage in a certain amount of preparation for each session. This includes becoming informed about the task in hand and thinking of ways of structuring the meeting so as to delegate some responsibility to group members and enlist their aid before and between meetings. Effective teaching requires that the teacher digest the information about the topic to be taught and plan how to present it to the learners "in their language" and on cue. Further, effective teachers are able to establish a give-and-take rapport with learners and to provide feedback and support in order to help group members to feel comfortable when talking, practicing, or demonstrating in the group. A supportive or therapeutic group leader has to reread logs or recordings of past sessions, look for evidence of nonparticipation by members who may need attention or for strong feelings or opinions that need exploration in future sessions, and be alert for patterns of interaction that seem to be developing. The supportive or therapeutic group leader is quite likely not to have an agenda or teaching plan in mind, but she is aware of potential problem areas and moves to intervene when appropriate. She must be willing and able to seek out assistance in understanding group processes; knowing when supervision from a more experienced group leader is needed is a very important quality for a group leader to have.

A sense of humor is also a great asset to a group leader. Despite adequate preparation for group sessions, unforeseen circumstances can disrupt the best-laid plans. Being able to detect the humor in unexpected situations allows the group leader to ride with the ebb and flow of group processes without becoming irritated, angry, punitive, or withdrawn. Such a leader can often use humor as a way of decreasing group tension levels.

In theory, nurses promote independent action in clients and patients, but, in practice, nurses "do for" patients in many instances and are comfortable in the role of authority or expert. In a group setting, the nurse who can promote independence and more effective behavior and encourage group members to be more responsible for what takes place in the group will be the more effective group leader. However, in the beginning she will need to set limits on who will be part of the group, where the group will meet, and what topics will be discussed. She will also need to decide how group members will be prepared to enter the group. These somewhat competing goals of fostering independence yet structuring the group require a blend of skill that can be acquired through practice in group leadership and through the study of group processes.

Another asset of the effective group leader is the ability to blend her own style of relating to constructive communication techniques. Some leaders may feel that asking, "What's with Betty and Tom?" seems too informal, even rude. Others may feel that saying, "It seems the group has some feeling about what John said" sounds stilted or too formal. Group leaders develop their own choice of words and their own ways of conveying the same idea. Learning to apply communication principles in a clear, direct manner takes quite a bit of practice.

The group leader's willingness to examine her own expectations for the group and to deal with them realistically is an important aspect of group leadership. She may deny wanting the group to proceed in a certain way, yet feel quite frustrated when it does not proceed as she expected. For example, the nurse leader of a health discussion group may have in mind that ten preplanned health topics will be covered in ten weeks. If the group members have many questions, cannot absorb the information, or are concerned about other issues, the group will probably not proceed as the leader expected, and she is then likely to react with anxiety, frustration, anger, and resentment. Effective group leadership requires that the nurse examine her own expectations and acquire the ability to correct or change them if they turn out to be unrealistic. This may evoke further anxiety in the nurse leader, but it is a necessary side effect of learning.

EFFECTIVE AND INEFFECTIVE GROUPS

According to Johnson and Johnson (1975), an effective group is one that accomplishes its task(s), meets interpersonal needs, and develops and grows in effectiveness. Effective groups are even capable of changing goals and matching individual needs to group goals. The nurse leader is aware of how effective groups work and strives to promote behaviors that lead to effective functioning. In order to accomplish their task, all group members must be aware of exactly what this task is.

In ineffective groups the goals are unclear, the group remains uninvolved or uninterested, and the given tasks often seem to promote competition rather than cooperation and collaboration.

In effective groups, communication between the leader and the group members and between the group members themselves is open, direct, and clear. Accurate expression of thoughts and feelings is encouraged. Individuality is supported, while activities that foster a closer working relationship and enhance the "common good" are encouraged. In such groups a high level of trust, support, safety, creativity, and constructive controversy is evident.

In ineffective groups, communication is usually a one-way affair, from the leader to the group. Ideas are expressed, while feelings are denied or ignored. No attempt is made to involve group members in group functions. The emphasis is on conformity, and the leaders seem most interested in the control of the group, in making sure that there is order and stability, and in maintaining the status quo.

Power and leadership are shared by all members in effective groups. The leader teaches the group members how to be effective, and members participate in decisions according to their ability. Controversy and conflict are assessed as possible clues to involvement and interest in the task. Members learn how to recognize problems and how to solve them with a minimum of energy and a maximum of satisfaction; they also learn how to evaluate the effectiveness of their solutions and, finally, the effectiveness of their group.

The leadership in ineffective groups is often based on seniority or authority. Participation of members is unequal; authoritarian members dominate the group and make the decisions. Controversy and conflict are ignored, avoided, or squelched. Group members do not learn how to solve problems or how to evaluate their effectiveness as group members or as a group. The status quo is maintained.

In summary, the group leader promotes effective functioning by:

clarifying the group task

changing the group task to match individual and group goals (when necessary)

promoting collaboration and cooperation

promoting security, trust, support, and creativity

encouraging constructive controversy

teaching group members to share leadership and responsibility in the group

teaching group members to problem-solve and to evaluate group functioning and resultant outcomes

WAYS OF LEARNING ABOUT GROUP FUNCTION

Learning to be an effective group leader cannot be accomplished merely by reading about group concepts and processes. An effective group leader has to have not only the theoretical knowledge about how groups work, but also the ability to assess group concepts and processes and to intervene in real-life groups. Assessing and intervening in group processes requires practice that should be supervised by an experienced leader.

One way to learn about group functioning is to join a task, teaching, or supportive or therapeutic group. As a participant, the nurse can begin to observe and study group concepts and processes in action. She might also be able to study group processes more effectively by becoming an observer/reporter for the group. In this role she would focus all her energies on listening and recording and would not participate verbally in the group interaction.

Prior to intervening in real-life group situations, the nurse can practice interacting in simulated situations; these have many learning advantages that real-life situations do not have. First, simulations contain less risk than real-life situations; learners know they are only "pretending." Less risk in simulations can often lead to less anxiety about an unknown situation, and to more potential for learning. Second, simulations allow learners to receive feedback for group behavior and skills; they can observe the consequences of their behavior without being so concerned about disclosing their feelings, receiving disapproval from authority figures, or psychologically "damaging" patients. Third, since group simulations are structured to contain elements of possible real-life group situations, experience in simulation is likely to increase one's ability to handle real situations more easily. Fourth, simulations are a "fun" way to learn, and motivation is usually high. By practicing some or all of the group simulations found at the ends of the first six chapters of this book, the nurse who is preparing to become a group leader can achieve all four of these benefits.

The next step in learning to be an effective group leader is actual practice in assessing and intervening in group process. This can occur through taking the role of designated group leader either in a new group or in an already established group of patients, clients, families, or health personnel. Being designated leader requires the output of more energy and the assumption of more responsibility, at least initially, than does assuming a group member role, a recorder role, or an observer role. Ultimately, the designated leader in an effective group shares responsibility and teaches group members how to assume responsibility for group decisions. The nurse can also practice being a group leader by taking the informal leader role in a group; once the learner is aware of how and when to intervene, she can assume formal leadership functions in a group.

SIMULATED EXERCISES

Each of the three simulated exercises that follow includes an experiential and a discussion component. When using Exercises 2 and 3, large groups should be divided into subgroups of not more than 15 members. Following the simulation, the entire group reconvenes for the discussion.

Ample space should be provided for subgroups to spread out, and chairs should be movable. When subgroups are too close there is a tendency to listen to others' discussions.

Exercise 1
Perceived Problems of Being in a Group

Objectives

1. To provide practice as leader, recorder, and listener in groups.

2. To compare and contrast the listening and telling skills of various participants.

3. To examine common concerns regarding being in group situations.

Procedure

1. The group or the instructor appoints a timekeeper.

2. The group or the instructor appoints a leader who directs the exercise.

3. The leader says, "Arrange yourselves into subgroups of three. One will be the recorder who writes down what is said, one will be the listener, and one will be the speaker who tells what problems she faces in group situations." (Variation: have the speaker tell what problems she anticipates as group leader.)

4. When the small subgroups are arranged, the leader asks the timekeeper to call time when 15 minutes are up. The leader gives the signal to begin.

5. When the timekeeper calls time, the groups scramble, so that each person plays a different role for the next 15 minutes.

6. When the timekeeper calls time, the entire group convenes for a group discussion.

7. The group may appoint a leader to focus the discussion.

8. The leader asks the timekeeper to remind the group when only 10 minutes remain for discussion. Generally, 25 to 50 minutes is an adequate length of time to cover the issues, but the amount of time required will increase with an increase in the size of the group.

9. The following issues can be used as topics for discussion:
   a. What did the recorders in each group observe?
   b. What helpful or not helpful attitudes did the speakers in each group perceive in their listeners, i.e., nonverbal clues of attention, support, boredom, etc.?
   c. What did the listeners observe about the speakers?
   d. How does a listener encourage a speaker to speak?
   e. What skills are required by a recorder as compared to a speaker or listener?
   f. Did the recorder interfere with speaking and/or listening; if so, in what way?

g. What concerns were expressed about being in (or leading) a group?
   (These may be written on a chalkboard or shown in overhead
   projection transparencies and used for reference purposes.)
h. How could each concern be handled in the most effective way?
   (Refer to Chapters 1-3 and 5 for specific interventions.)
i. How can what was learned in this excercise be applied in actual
   group situations?

Exercise 2

Introductions

This exercise is designed to give the nurse leader practical experience in giving, hearing, and analyzing group introductions without the risks that would be involved in actual patient or staff group situations.

Objectives

1. To practice introducing self to others.

2. To observe how others present themselves to the group.

3. To observe group processes characteristic of the orientation phase of groups.

Procedure

1. The group or instructor appoints a timekeeper. The timekeeper makes sure that each person's introduction does not exceed three minutes. Whenever a group member takes more than three minutes, the timekeeper turns to the next member and says, "Next, please."

2. The group or the instructor appoints a leader for each group.

3. The group leader appoints a recorder from among his group members. The recorder is asked to jot down observations regarding how people introduce themselves, how group members react toward being asked to introduce themselves, and the level of and changes in group cohesiveness.

4. The group leader asks the group members, "Will each of you introduce yourself to the group, say what you do, who you are as a person, and why you are participating in this exercise? Who will start?"

5. When all group members, including the leader, have introduced themselves, the entire group convenes.

6. A discussion leader volunteers or is appointed by the group. This leader asks the recorder to assist by helping the group to present their observations concerning the following issues:
   a. Did people tend to use socially acceptable, rational introductions? If so, is this characteristic of the orientation phase of a group? If not, what explanations do the group have for the presence or lack of more openness?
   b. Do nurses seem more likely to stereotype themselves than others might? Why?
   c. Why do people seem hesitant and cautious about expressing themselves in the group? If some people gave too much personal information, what might be an explanation for that type of behavior?

d. Did group members really seem to get acquainted during the introductions? Why, or why not?

e. What information seems most helpful for the leader to give during her introduction?

f. What information seems most helpful for group members to give other group members during introductions?

g. How can what was learned in this exercise be applied to actual group situations?

Variation: Two leaders can work together to lead the discussion. In this case, the following discussion question can be added:

h. What advantages and disadvantages were there to coleadership? (Refer to Chapter 5.)

Exercise 3

Paraphrasing

This exercise provides practice in listening to and restating what others say.
Many times the receiver of a message makes judgments about what the other
has said and responds to these judgments rather than to the other's message.
Because effective leadership requires expert listening and restating skills, this
exercise can be redone whenever the group leader begins to notice a tendency
toward interpreting group members' messages without sufficient basis for the
interpretation.

Procedure

1. The group or the instructor appoints a timekeeper, who is to make
   sure that time limits set for each step are kept; the timekeeper
   also is to remind the group at appropriate intervals how much
   time remains.

2. The group decides on time limits for each step.

3. The group or the instructor appoints a leader for each group.

4. Each member is asked to talk about the best thing that happened
   to him this week. One member starts by telling the person who
   sits to his right in the group the best thing that happened to him.
   The second person paraphrases what the first person has said, using
   different words to describe what happened. The exercise continues
   in this manner, with one person recounting the best thing that
   happened to him, and the next person paraphrasing, followed by
   another person telling her best experience and another person
   paraphrasing that experience until everyone has either told or
   paraphrased.

15-30
minutes

5. The leader then asks group members to reverse roles and have the
   person who told of the experience become the paraphraser.

6. The entire group discusses the following points:

15-30
minutes

   a. What is difficult about paraphrasing another person's statements?
   b. Who in the group found it easier to tell a story as opposed to
      paraphrasing someone else's? Who found the reverse to be true?
      What ideas do the group have about why this might occur?
   c. What was learned from this exercise that can be applied in
      real-life group situations?

READINGS

Clark, Carolyn C. "A Comparison of Learning Outcomes for Teacher and Student Players in a Peer-Mediated, Simulation Game for Associate Degree Nursing Students," *Fourteenth Annual NASAGA Conference Proceedings.* Los Angeles: University of Southern California Press, 1976.

Johnson, Davis, and Frank Johnson. *Joining Together: Group Theory and Group Skills.* Englewood Cliffs, N.J.: Prentice-Hall, 1975.

Laird, Mona. "Techniques for Teaching Pre- and Postoperative Patients," *American Journal of Nursing* 75(1975): 1338-1340.

Mezannotte, E. "Group Instruction in Preparation for Surgery," *American Journal of Nursing* 70(1970): 89-91.

Ramshorn, Mary. "The Group as a Therapeutic Tool," *Perspectives in Psychiatric Care* 8(1970): 104-105.

Rosini, L.A., and others. "Group Meetings in a Pediatric Intensive Care Unit," *Pediatrics* 53(1974): 371-374.

Salzer, Joan. "Classes to Improve Diabetic Self-Care," *American Journal of Nursing* 75(1975): 1324-1326.

Smith, E.D. "Group Conferences for Postpartum Patients," *American Journal of Nursing* 71(1971): 112-113.

Wittes, Glorianne, and Norma Radin. "Two Approaches to Group Work with Parents in a Compensatory Pre-School Program," *Social Work* 16(1971): 42-50.

2

Group Concepts and Process

GROUP CONTENT AND PROCESS

Content, or group content, are terms used to describe topics discussed in a group session. Content may be straightforward and explicit, or it may convey a symbolic meaning. Both explicit and symbolic meanings are assessed when one group member comments, "Boy, is it hot in here!" at a time when other group members are arguing with one another. Overtly, the room may be warm temperature-wise; symbolically, the group member may be commenting on the "hot" issue being discussed. With practice, an experienced leader can tune into both straightforward and symbolic meanings being expressed in the group.

In groups there is constant movement toward and away from the goal as group members seek to reduce the tension that arises when people attempt to have their individual needs met, yet engage in group tasks or interactions. This movement is referred to as group process. Because so much activity occurs in some groups, the inexperienced leader often has difficulty identifying group process. In the group process approach the leader assumes that the group is not only an aggregate of individuals, but a dynamic, ever-changing ebb and flow of tension. When tension levels are too high or too low, group process is impeded. For each group the leader must be able to identify what group processes are occurring, what will impede and what will assist group process, when to intervene in the process, and when to remain silent.

The following excerpt from an adolescent health discussion group points up the leader's lack of awareness of group process and shows how he impedes effective group movement:

> Leader: "You guys shouldn't drink, you know."
> Tony: "What do you know about it?"
> Leader: "Drinking is bad for your health."
> Tony: "That's what everyone says."
> Leader: "So why not listen?"
> Tony (burps loudly):   "Pass the beer, please."
> Sam: "Enough talk for today."
> Leader: "O.K., since you don't want to talk, we'll end for today."

Here, the leader seems to be at war with the group and tries to use logic to convince the members that drinking is unhealthy. Had the leader realized that the members of this group would be likely to resist logical arguments (which they would probably have heard before from authority figures), he might have taken a different tack, such as asking them what drinking did for them, what they knew about the physiological effects of alcohol, or even whether they thought that he would tell them what everyone else had told them. In this way, the leader might have decreased group resistance to his statements and possibly begun to convince the group that he was interested in listening to them and understanding their perceptions. By taking such a role, he would not only potentially reduce group tension, but also serve as a role model for effective group interaction.

As a group leader continues to observe group process over time, he will find it useful to ask himself a few questions:

What seems to lead to increased tension levels?
What indicates conflict?

When does the group seem to be apathetic?
How are decisions arrived at?
What types of leadership occur?
What rules for behavior are in operation?
What factors lead to effective movement toward and away
from group goals?
What signs of aggression and assertiveness are evident?
What phase of group process does the group seem to be in?
What themes recur?

TENSION AND ANXIETY IN THE GROUP

At times, all group members, including the leader, show signs of
tension or anxiety. Mild and even moderate anxiety can be useful in promoting group movement. When the tension level becomes too high, the leader takes steps to lower it, after noting
which indicants of anxiety increase and which decrease, and at
what points during the session this happens.

Anxiety is an unexplained feeling of discomfort that one
experiences when expectations are not met. New group members
may experience anxiety when they expect the group experience
to be of one sort, and it turns out to be something else. Group
members can also experience anxiety when asked questions
about any topic on which they lack information or feel unsure
of themselves. For example, a group member who is obese may
experience anxiety when diet is discussed, and a group leader
who does not have correct information on a certain drug may
feel anxious when asked to discuss that drug. Anxiety is a common reaction in unfamiliar or new situations; the first meeting
of a group may result in such feelings in both group members
and the leader. Some people are quite sensitive to disapproval
and may feel anxious when the leader or other group members
indicate disapproval of their words or actions. Any situation
that interferes with basic needs can create anxiety. Not being
respected or recognized can lead to feelings of anxiety; leaders
who are challenged by group members or group members who

are called by inappropriate or incorrect names may experience anxiety.

Signs of anxiety include restlessness, lack of eye contact, body tenseness, stiff or repetitive gestures, rapid shallow breathing, perspiration, rapid or unclear speech, changing the topic of conversation, silence, and distorting or overreacting to others' comments.

The group leader can follow several procedures to reduce anxiety in new group members. First, spending time with the members prior to the first group session will help them feel more comfortable, because they will then know at least one person who will be in the group. Also, the leader can share with the group members the reasons why she is leading the group and what her feelings are at that moment. Admission of her own feelings of tension or anxiety about starting a new group will often help the members to feel more comfortable in sharing their own thoughts and feelings. The leader can anticipate that in an unknown situation group members will be curious about what role she will play. By inviting comments from the group about what they expect of the leader and by stating specifically the functions the leader plans to perform she can decrease tension.

Warming-up exercises may be quite helpful in decreasing anxiety in a new group. One exercise consists of having each member write down and/or verbally explain the reason he is there and what he hopes to get from the group experience. Or, to get the group started, the members can be asked to draw pictures of themselves and then pair off to talk about their drawings and possibly to express their fears about being in the group. Films and other audiovisual materials can be used to stimulate discussion. The innovative leader can devise many such warming-up exercises.

When group members are unable to talk about their discomfort, yet the leader senses that tension is high, she can make a comment such as, "It seems we're all a little tense," or "I guess we're all a little nervous since we don't know each other yet," or "I sense this subject worries you," or "This is hard to learn, but it will be worth the effort."

Group leaders can prepare themselves for meeting anxiety-provoking situations as they arise. One way to do this is to think through, or even write down, a summary of what one expects to happen in the coming session. This technique will help identify hidden fears, and once this is accomplished further self-questioning can include such queries as: "So what if that does happen?" "What could I do to handle that if it did occur?"

Role-playing can also be used to decrease anxiety. Suppose a group member becomes anxious when asking for a raise, when setting a limit on a child's behavior, or when asking for a favor. Two group members, or the leader and one group member, can preplay the problematic situation; then the two role players can exchange roles to find out how it feels to "be in the other's shoes." Group members can serve as coaches to the role players and give feedback after the role play about how the situation could best have been handled.

Relaxation exercises can also be used to decrease anxiety. The first step is consciously to contract and then relax the various body muscles. This allows the learner to "get the feel of" tension and relaxation. Next, he imagines a pleasant scene. When he is completely relaxed, the anxiety-provoking situation is called to his attention, and, as soon as he feels his body becoming tense, he is asked to focus again on relaxing his muscles and imagining the pleasant scene. With practice, the learner will be able to go through an entire tension-provoking scene mentally without experiencing overwhelming anxiety. Once he has mastered relaxation in role-playing situations, he can practice the exercise in actual anxiety-provoking experiences (Fensterheim, 1971).

Finally, humor can be used to dissipate tension. However, it should be used cautiously so that group members are not made to feel degraded, and it should never be used to avoid confronting important issues.

GROUP CONFLICT

Conflict caused by opposing forces within the group can occur in an individual member, or it can be shared by subgroups or by the entire group. An individual can experience conflict within himself when he wishes to be singled out for special treatment by the leader yet at the same time fears the leader's disapproval; this conflict can be resolved when the individual conforms to the behavior of the other group members. Another solution to bids for special attention by one group member is for the group to take over and interfere with the attention-getting behavior.

Sources of conflict in the group as a whole include being given an impossible task, having conflicting loyalties within and outside the group, jockeying for power or status, dislike of one another, and involvement in the task assigned. Whether the group leader should intervene in a group conflict depends on whether group process seems to be impeded or assisted by it. Intervention may be necessary when some group members attack others' ideas before they are completely expressed, take sides and refuse to compromise, attack one another's personal attributes or behavior, insist that the group does not have the knowledge or experience to resolve their difficulties, or accuse one another of not understanding. Whenever any of these symptoms of conflict occur, the leader may intervene by stating the group goal more clearly, defining smaller steps that can be taken to assure obtaining the goal, suggesting that more time be allowed to achieve the goal, teaching the group what they need to know to reach their goal, finding a goal that interests all members, requiring members to substitute a statement such as, "I feel angry when people tease me" for "You teased me, you rat!" and asking group members to paraphrase others' comments in order to decrease distortion of communication messages.

When group members appear not to understand the group goal, frequently disagree, and show strong positive or negative feeling and signs of impatience, the group leader will probably not want to interfere, since these are signs of conflict arising from involvement in the task.

GROUP APATHY

When group members show indifference to the task, appear bored, and seem unable to mobilize their energies or to persevere, they may be using apathy to deal with high anxiety. An apathetic response is a withdrawal reaction; it can be used as a disguise for tension and discomfort.

The group leader needs to intervene whenever the following signs of apathy are noted: tardiness, absenteeism, attempts to end meetings early, minimal participation by group members, frequent yawns, dragging conversation, loss of the point of a discussion, reluctance to assume responsibility for group functioning, precipitous decisions, failure to carry through on decisions, or lack of preparation for coming meetings.

The leader needs to determine the source of apathy before intervening. She might ask the group members such questions as:

What do you think about the group goal?
Do you feel the group goal is relevant?
What meaning does the goal have for you?
What do you think will happen if you attain the goal?
Do you think the group atmosphere lends itself to sharing and cooperation?
Do you have the skills you need to communicate easily with one another?
Is effort toward achieving the group goal clearly organized and coordinated?
Have you been asked to make decisions you think will not be acted upon?
Do you think I make unilateral decisions?
Does conflict between a few members overshadow group movement toward the goal?

Once the source of apathy has been identified, the leader can act to overcome it. If the task goal was imposed by others or by the leader, the group can be helped to decide on a goal that the members consider more relevant. If group members fear punishment, the leader can help the group to explore whether this fear is realistic; if it is, perhaps the leader's expectations need to be reexamined. If group atmosphere is too tense, or if the room is crowded, noisy, poorly ventilated, or otherwise not conducive to effective group interaction, the leader is responsible for modifying the milieu. If the group lacks communication skills, these can be taught through the use of the simulated group exercises at the ends of the chapters of this book and by role modeling effective communication behavior. If efforts toward achievement of the group goal are not clearly organized or co-ordinated, the leader may wish to rethink her approaches and/or seek supervision from a more experienced group leader. If decision making leads to meaningless or unilateral decisions, the leader needs to teach the group more effective ways of arriving at meaningful decisions. If conflict overshadows group movement toward its goal, the leader must determine the sources of the conflict and intervene appropriately.

DECISION MAKING

Some decisions about group functioning are usually made by the group leader. Decisions about when, where, and how often the group will meet, how long meetings will last, and what the behavior limits will be are the responsibility of the designated nurse leader. The nurse who leads a group as a private practitioner must also decide on the fee for her service. It is not usually feasible to open such decisions to group decision making, although the wise leader does allow group members to express their reactions to these decisions.

Decision making by the group members occurs most frequently in task groups. Some decisions with which a task group might become involved include planning group activities; deciding whether to allow more—or less—time for a specific topic or problem to be discussed; deciding on the topic for the next week's discussion; and deciding how to handle group members who monopolize the conversation, pick on other group members, are silent, are new to the group, or are leaving the group.

Many groups will need to learn from the leader how to make effective group decisions by consensus. The first step in this process is for the leader to state the overall problem in clear and easily understandable terms. Next, the leader clarifies and elaborates on the various aspects of the problem. She then encourages group members to develop alternate solutions to the problem and even seeks out differences of opinion, since disagreement can assist the group to arrive at an effective decision when a wide range of information is presented. Throughout the decision-making process, the leader helps to keep the discussion relevant by making statements such as, "We're off the track now," or "Let's get back to suggesting solutions," or "We are discussing .... now." Another step in effective decision making is to summarize the alternative solutions; this can be done verbally, or the suggested solutions can be written on a chalkboard or recorded by a group secretary or recorder. After summarizing the possible solutions, the group can test them out verbally and/or through action. As a decision emerges, the leader queries group members' commitment to it. For example, she might say, "It seems that the logical solution is . . . . What do each of you think of it?" The final step in the process is for the group to reach a consensus on the decision. Admittedly, arriving at decisions by this process is an ideal to be striven for; rarely will it be completely realized. However, one important result is that the group members are introduced to the process and the skills used to make effective decisions by consensus.

LEADERSHIP SKILLS

At one time, leadership was thought to be an attribute that, like charisma, was possessed naturally by certain special individuals. Now it seems more useful to think of group leadership in terms of a number of functions that need to be performed by some member in the group; the designated leader may, in fact, fulfill some, all, or none of these functions. From this viewpoint, the nurse can be seen as a group leader whenever she fulfills needed group functions. Thus, the nurse can be a group leader in a group for which the designated leader is a physician, a nursing supervisor, or some other authority figure.

Leadership functions are of two types: task functions and maintenance functions. Regardless of the type of group, both types of functions must be fulfilled in order for the group to work at its highest possible level of performance.

Task functions are directly related to the accomplishment of group goals; they include the following leader behaviors:

1. Getting the group going—
    e.g., "Let's get started."
2. Keeping the group moving toward its goal—
    e.g., "Let's get on with our discussion of . . . ."
3. Clarifying unclear statements or behaviors—
    e.g., "I'm not sure I understood your idea, could you tell us in another way?"
4. Suggesting ways to move toward the goal—
    e.g., "We could spend a few minutes sorting this out before we move on to another topic."
5. Pointing out movement toward or away from the goal—
    e.g., "So far we've finished . . . but still need to tackle the problem of . . . ."
6. Restating more clearly what others have said—
    e.g., "Let me summarize what I heard you saying . . . ."
7. Refocusing discussion on the task or on a small step toward the goal—
    e.g., "First let's work on . . . , then . . . , the next step of . . . ."
8. Giving information—
    e.g., "The group will meet from 8 to 9 p.m."

Maintenance functions are directly related to improving interpersonal relationships within the group and may include the following leader behaviors:

1. Giving support to group members who are unsure or anxious—
   e.g., "I guess you're upset about this, but give it a try."
2. Relieving extreme tension levels—
   e.g., "Let's role play this situation."
3. Encouraging direct communication—
   e.g., "Tell Mr. West what you were telling me, Mrs. Swanson."
4. Voicing group feeling—
   e.g., "I sense the group is worried about this."
5. Agreeing or accepting—
   e.g., "That's a good point."
6. Helping the group to evaluate itself—
   e.g., "Let's all tell what we've gotten from this group experience."

In general, leadership skills are enhanced by using certain communication techniques. For example, paraphrasing, which involves restating what another person has said, gives the message "I care about what you said so I want to make sure I understand your idea." It is useful to preface one's remarks with a statement such as, "If I understood you, you said . . ." and "Did I read you right? Your idea is . . . ."

Behavior description involves stating only what was observed without commenting on the meaning or motive for the behavior. Behavior descriptions include statements such as, "Everyone talked today," "You interrupted Jane three times today," and "You already told us about your opinions today, John." Statements such as, "You must be angry," or "Why don't you listen to me?" or "You're just like my sister," are not behavioral descriptions, and they are likely to create discomfort and defensiveness in others.

Feeling description involves a direct statement of how one feels. One who uses this communication technique must feel safe and secure in the group, since sharing feelings implies a risk. Direct expressions of feeling include such comments as, "I'm nervous," "I'm angry," "I feel happy," and "I like you." Indirect expression of feelings is open to misinterpretation by others and should be avoided by group leaders. Some indirect feeling expressions are blushing when embarrassed, saying nothing or attacking a group member when angry or anxious, and changing the subject or the rules when irritated.

Validating is a technique that includes checking with others in a tentative way to see whether one's perceptions are correct. Paraphrasing has to do with verbal statements, while validating has more to do with hunches, feelings, and nonverbal processes. When attempting to validate, the leader avoids showing approval or disapproval of behavior and merely checks out perceptions. Validating statements include such comments as, "You seem nervous; are you?" and "I sense you're angry with me; am I right?" The leader never assumes that her perceptions are correct without checking them out; statements such as, "Why are you angry?" and "Why didn't you . . . ?" should not be used before validating that the person is angry or did not follow through.

Feedback refers to letting group members know how they affect each other. Feedback is most helpful when it is specific, concrete, and based on empathy rather than on the leader's need to appear in charge. Examples of this technique are, "You've talked a lot today; let someone else talk," and "You've asked that question four times; what's that all about?"

NORMS AND COHESIVENESS

Norms are rules for behavior within the group. Each member will bring to the group his own ideas about appropriate behavior with others. If group members are drawn from highly divergent social, economic, educational, or cultural groups, it may take quite a while for them to agree on appropriate group behavior.

Despite the attitudes the individual members contribute, certain norms will be developed spontaneously within the group. Because norms refer to expected behavior, they carry a "should" or "ought to" quality, and some beliefs may be carryovers from childhood experiences. The leader may set a rule for behavior, but the group will accept it only when the behavior it calls for is rewarded and enforced by other group members.

The group leader can use several techniques in establishing norms. She can look for the presence of already existing norms and for norms that seem to be developing. Norms can be initiated by the leader who may suggest, "I think we should share our thoughts and feelings now." She can have an even stronger influence on group norms by demonstrating, through her own behavior, what appropriate group behavior is. Instead of merely suggesting that others share their thoughts and feelings, the group leader might share her own. This would allow others to see that it is safe to express themselves and would also serve as a model for expressing oneself in the group context. The leader shares feelings when it seems to be helpful to group process and refrains from doing so when the expression would simply serve to meet the leader's needs for attention, sympathy, or retaliation.

Norms can work in favor of or against group cohesion. Cohesiveness is the attraction of the group members for each other. Highly cohesive groups are motivated to work effectively toward group goals and to satisfy all members' interpersonal needs. The more favorable the expectations are that members have about group membership, the more attractive will the idea of group membership be. The leader can influence attraction to the group by making sure that everyone has the same goals in mind, that group goals are relevant and clearly stated, that paths to goal attainment are known and rewarded, and that cooperation among members is promoted.

Some measures of cohesiveness are arrival on time, full attendance at group meetings, a high trust and support level within the group, the ability of the group to tolerate individuality and have fun, the ability to work cooperatively with other group members to enforce agreed-upon norms, and ease in making statements of liking for the group or for group members.

Groups cannot become highly cohesive unless all members, including the leader, interact on an equal basis. The leader can increase cohesiveness by helping group members to feel part of and equal within the group, by controlling group functioning effectively, and by teaching members how to give and get satisfaction or affection from working with each other. The leader should try to include all group members in the discussions by asking for everyone's opinion and by seeing withdrawn or silent members individually between meetings to discover their reasons for nonparticipation. The more frequently group members interact with each other, the more likely it is that the group will become cohesive. To promote group interaction, the leader may deflect some of the questions from herself to a group member. Frequency of group meetings can also affect cohesiveness, since the more frequently a group meets, the higher the potential for interaction; the leader may consider increasing the frequency of the meetings if other attempts to promote cohesiveness fail. Another way to influence cohesiveness is to help the group to identify similarities that exist between members; this technique increases a sense of community in group members.

Group cohesiveness is strongly influenced by the balance between members' needs to control others in the group. This need ranges from wanting to control all aspects of everyone else's behavior to abdicating control entirely because the situation is unsafe or unhealthy. When leadership is shared by all group members, all will learn to control some aspects of group functioning and to accept control in others. The leader demonstrates appropriate control levels by structuring the group, yet allowing it to assume responsibility for some decisions.

The leader can increase affection among group members and feelings of satisfaction or pride in accomplishment by planning meetings so that the potential for success is high. To do this, the leader does not place group members "on the spot" by requiring them to answer after they have stated that they do not feel like talking at that time, and she does not allow others to do so. She rewards group members for cooperation and goal attainment by commenting on goals reached and not by commenting on poor performance except, perhaps, to suggest additional ways of attaining the goal.

Allowing group members to express hostility and conflict will also increase cohesiveness. Unless anger or resentment are openly expressed, they will go underground and impede member cooperation and interaction. The group leader conveys the idea, directly and indirectly, that it is "O.K. to talk about anger and differences here."

PHASES OF GROUP MOVEMENT

The phases of group movement may be classified according to several systems. Perhaps the simplest system divides the group into three phases: orientation, working, and termination. During the orientation phase, group members are seeking to be accepted in the group and to find out how they are similar to and different from the other members. Their expectations for outcomes of group experiences are often unrealistic. For example, it is highly unlikely that long-term behaviors will be changed by four to six sessions of a supportive group. And certainly expecting to be cured of cancer in a supportive group is totally unrealistic. Anxiety is high during this phase, and there are frequent bids for the leader to perform unreasonable feats and to be all things to all group members. The leader may have to be quite verbal in the first few meetings as she teaches group members how to relate to one another and how to move toward the group goal. As the group proceeds, members may directly or indirectly express anger toward the leader for not being able to meet all their needs. It is important that the leader stick to realistic goals, while at the same time assisting group members to express their thoughts and feelings regarding what happens in the group.

During the working phase, when the group has learned to work together cooperatively, the leader needs to intervene less frequently. Leadership functions are shared. Positive and negative feelings may be expressed, control issues are worked out to the satisfaction of all, cohesiveness increases, norms are solidified and reinforced, and progress is made toward attaining the group goal.

The focus in the termination phase is on evaluating and summarizing the group experience. Feelings of sadness, satisfaction, frustration or anger, guilt, and rejection or denial of feeling may occur. The longer the group has been together, the more intense and extended will be the termination phase. In any one session, groups may show behavior characteristic of all three phases.

THEMES

Although many topics may be discussed by a given group or even in one group session, one predominant theme can usually be identified. At first, it may seem that group meetings are disconnected and that the subjects discussed or the activities pursued are unrelated. Yet a pervading theme can often be identified. It may not necessarily be logical or overt; it may be implied through association, symbolic meaning, or feeling tone. For example, one group of nursing-home residents kept returning to the topic of exploitation of nursing-home patients for the financial benefit of the government, and how change was needed; all the group members became animatedly involved in the discussion whenever this topic came up. On one level, a discussion of this kind could be taken at its surface value; on another level, the leader in this instance became aware that nursing-home residents felt exploited and used by society and even perhaps by the nursing-home staff.

The feeling of being exploited, mistreated, and used is a common theme in group sessions in long-term institutions such as psychiatric hospitals and prisons. The feeling of being different occurs as a theme in group sessions when all members have the same illness or handicap. Prenatal discussion groups may have themes of fear of pain and of the birth experience. Groups composed of people who are all at a particular stage of growth and development may exhibit themes characteristic of that period; for example, four- to six-year-olds in a group may have a theme of competition, while an eight- to eleven-year-old group may have a theme of industry.

Not every group will have one of these common themes. The group leader needs to be attuned to the possible linkages and underlying consistent meaning of what is expressed in group interaction that may imply a theme or ongoing group concern.

SIMULATED EXERCISES

Each of the two simulated exercises that follow includes an experiential and a discussion section. If the group is large, it should be divided into subgroups of not more than 15 members. Following the simulation, the entire group reconvenes for a discussion period. If either exercise is completed without an instructor or supervisor present, participants should plan to share difficulties and insights with an experienced group leader following completion of the exercise.

Exercise 1

Sharing with Others

This exercise gives the learner the opportunity to practice sharing information about herself in a nonthreatening environment and to learn to listen to other group members who also share information about themselves. It also provides an opportunity for the learner to observe how sharing can influence group cohesiveness.

Objectives

1. To develop skill in sharing information about self with others.

2. To develop a recognition of safe levels of self-disclosure.

3. To learn to listen to what others wish to say without prodding or debating.

Procedure

1. The group decides the time limits for each section of the exercise.

2. The group or the instructor appoints a timekeeper, who makes sure that time limits for each section are observed. The timekeeper also reminds the group at appropriate intervals how much time remains.

3. The group or the instructor appoints a leader for each subgroup.

10 minutes per person maximum

4. The subgroup leaders ask each of their group members to write down three questions she would like to be asked by others. Questions should deal with interests, hobbies, family, friends, beliefs, hopes, goals in life, or activities. Each person writes down her three questions, signs her name, and passes the paper to the subgroup leader, who asks each member to answer her own three questions. The leader makes sure that personal information is shared and discussed on a voluntary basis. Whenever the group member feels like going on to another question, she is free to do so. There is to be no argument or debate. Each person is free to state her position without argument from others.

15–30 minutes

5. When all group members have been asked their three questions, the subgroup leader asks each group member to tell one new thing she learned about every other group member.

15–30 minutes

6. The entire group then meets to discuss the following points:
   a. What was easy and what was difficult about this exercise?
   b. What was learned from this exercise that can be applied in other group situations?

Exercise 2
Decision-Making Conflict

This exercise gives the learner opportunity to practice in group decision making and in assessing conflict within a group.

Objectives

1. To develop skill in group decision making.

2. To develop skill in assessing symptoms of conflict within a group.

Procedure

1. The group or the instructor appoints a leader.

5–15 minutes

2. The leader appoints a timekeeper, whose duty is to assure that the task is finished in 20 minutes.

3. The leader locates two group members who agree to be observers for this simulation and gives them an instruction sheet to read. (See pp. 38 and 39.)

20 minutes

4. When the observers signal the leader that they are ready to begin, the leader reads the following task aloud:
"We are to take 20 minutes to decide on five criteria for mercy killing. When the timekeeper calls time, our observers will report to us what they have observed."

5. The timekeeper calls time at the end of 20 minutes.

6. The leader asks the observers to report their observations.

15–45 minutes

7. The leader then asks the group to discuss the following points:
   a. What could the leader have done to reduce conflict?
   b. What techniques could the leader have used to assist the decision-making process?
   c. What was learned from this exercise that can be applied in other group situations?

37

Observer 1

Your function is to look out for conflict in the group. Record examples of conflict as they occur, using the observation blank below. When you are sure that you understand the items listed on the observation blank, signal the group leader that you are ready to begin. When the group discussion is over, you will be asked to report your recorded observations to the entire group.

CONFLICT OBSERVATION BLANK

Symptoms   Example

members are impatient with each other

ideas are attacked before being completely expressed

members take sides and refuse to compromise

members disagree subtly

comments are made with strong feeling

members attack each other personally

members accuse others of not understanding

members hear distorted parts of others' speeches

members insist the group does not have
   the skill to solve the problem

members feel the group is too large
   or too small to work effectively

Conclusions: an impossible task; conflicting loyalties; status seeking;
                   personal dislikes; appropriate involvement in working toward
                   the goal

Observer 2

Your function is to look out for decision making in the group. Record examples of decision making as they occur, using the observation blank below. When you are sure that you understand the items listed on the observation blank, signal the group leader that you are ready to begin. When the group discussion is over, you will be asked to report your recorded observations to the entire group.

DECISION MAKING OBSERVATION BLANK

Steps in Decision Making   Example

states the problem

clarifies and elaborates

develops alternative solutions

keeps the discussion relevant

tests commitment to the emerging decision

summarizes

agrees to the decision

tests the consequences of solutions

READINGS

Bradford, Leland, Dorothy Stock, and Murray Horwitz. "How to Diagnose Group Problems," *Adult Leadership* 12(1953): 12-19.

Cartwright, Dorwin, and Alvin Zander. *Group Dynamics.* Evanston, Ill.: Row, Peterson and Co., 1953.

Epstein, Charlotte. *Effective Interaction in Contemporary Nursing.* Englewood Cliffs, N.J.: Prentice-Hall, 1974.

Fensterheim, Herbert. *Help Without Psychoanalysis.* New York: Stein and Day, 1971.

Glasser, Paul, Rosemary Sarri, and Robert Vintner, eds. *Individual Change Through Small Groups.* New York: Macmillan, 1974.

Johnson, Donald, and Frank Johnson. *Joining Together: Group Theory and Group Skills.* Englewood Cliffs, N.J.: Prentice-Hall, 1975.

Schmuck, Richard, and Patricia Schmuck, *Group Processes in the Classroom.* Dubuque, Iowa: William C. Brown Co., 1971.

Whitaker, Dorothy, and Morton Lieberman. *Psychotherapy Through Group Process.* New York: Atherton, 1964.

3

Special Group Problems

Among the more common group problems that the nurse leader will have to deal with are monopolizing, scapegoating, silence, the new member, transference and countertransference, physical aggression, nonverbal groups or group members, absences, and manipulation.

MONOPOLIZING

Groups are likely to have one member who talks excessively. In certain situations it may be reasonable to expect one member to do most or at least a major part of the talking in a group session. For example, when a group member is presenting special information to the group, it would be expected that that person would speak more than the others. However, when the purpose of the group is to share ideas, to learn from one another, or to make group decisions, a member who fails to let others contribute can impede group movement. Novice group leaders tend to become irritated by the overtalkative member and often fail to consider that such behavior occurs because other group members allow it to occur. Monopolizing can serve as a protective device for the group. The more silent group members may be anxious or fearful, or they may lack trust, and it is somewhat comforting to them that someone else will take responsibility for what happens in the group. At the same time, others in the group may show signs of irritation with the overtalkative person but have mixed feelings about quieting him. Meanwhile, the monopolizing person may also have mixed feelings about doing most of the talking. At first, he may be overtalkative in an effort to decrease his level of anxiety, or perhaps he may be seeking a special relationship with the leader or feel uncomfortable during silences. In time, though, he will no doubt feel even more uncomfortable by being the only one in the group who is talking. He may even resent other members for "forcing" him to take all the responsibility for what happens in the group. In fact, then, monopolizing is a group problem that arises when one group member agrees—on some level—with other group members to talk and thereby to protect them. Unfortunately, while monopolizing begins as a protective device for both the overtalkative member and the rest of the group, in the long run, resentment among the group members increases and group movement will decrease.

In such cases, the knowledgeable leader will intervene, using any of a number of interventions that have been found effective, so that group movement can occur. Which intervention the leader chooses will be based on her assessment of the reason for the talkative behavior and also on how effective a particular intervention might be. Not every intervention is effective in every group, and the leader may have to try several before she finds one that works in a specific instance. Also, the leader needs to consider her own feelings about the intervention she chooses. If she is not convinced that a technique can be helpful, it would be best not to use it; once negative leader expectations have been conveyed to the group, the intervention will be ineffective.

One source of monopolizing is the effort of one group member to convince others of the correctness or worthwhileness of his ideas. Sometimes an overtalkative member may go on and on merely because he does not sense that the others agree with him or accept his ideas. In such a case, the leader might provide opportunity for feedback with a remark such as "What does the group think about what John has been saying?" This will often quiet the overtalkative person.

Another source of overtalkativeness is the attempt of one member to interest the rest of the group in matters that are irrelevant to the purpose of the meeting. Here, the leader could intervene by polling for consensus about what the group considers relevant.

Yet another source is the attempt of one group member to meet his needs for recognition. If the leader concludes that this might be the difficulty, it would be wise for her to assess the group atmosphere to see whether it is marked by threat and competition rather than by warmth and support; if so, several techniques are available to the leader for decreasing anxiety and tension. Also, she might decide to see the overtalkative member between group sessions; this individual recognition might provide sufficient support to allow him to relinquish his need for verbal control of the group.

When the leader senses the support and potential strength of group members, she may try to elicit their assistance in dealing with the problem. She may say, "I think we need to look at why one person has been given responsibility for what happens here." This may draw forth statements from the group, for example, "I don't know what to say, so I let Alice talk." The monopolizing person might also admit that silence makes her uncomfortable. If the group members are able to verbalize their feelings, the leader can then work with these with such responses as, "It's quite normal for a person to feel at a loss for words when he is new to a group, but in time you'll feel more at ease here," or "Let's try to work out this problem of getting more people in the group to talk; what could we do to make the amount of talking more equal?"

Often groups are not cohesive or cooperative enough to respond effectively to this kind of intervention, otherwise monopolizing would not have developed in the first place. The leader may therefore have to intervene more directly by saying, "Stop talking, Fred; let's hear what Jim and Stacey have to say," or "Everyone in this group has a right to talk; does anyone else have a comment to make?" or "Let's move on to something else now."

If none of these tactics is effective, the leader might consider asking the monopolizing person to leave the group for five or ten minutes whenever he takes over all the talking. The "time out" technique must be used with caution, however, since it can be perceived as punishment. But it does place responsibility for talking with the remaining group members, and thus has potential for changing group interactions. Such a tactic is an example of behavior modification (see Chapter 6) and will probably work best when the leader is not overly irritated with the monopolizing person and rewards him each time his overtalking decreases.

SCAPEGOATING

Scapegoating is a process whereby one or two members of the group are singled out and agree, consciously or unconsciously, to be the targets for group hostility or advice. Many times the behavior of those scapegoated has become irritating; however, there are ways for the group to deal with such behavior without resorting to hostility.

The use of a scapegoat is a convenient way for the group to negate responsibility for what happens in the group. Simply by blaming someone else, the members of the group can decrease their own anxiety and ignore their responsibility. Frequently, the scapegoated member sets up situations that evoke the group's anger. Sometimes the group is really angry with the leader for not fulfilling their unrealistic expectations, but rather than displeasing the leader, members "take out" their anger on the scapegoat. They may also scapegoat one member because they themselves feel worthless or inept and can concretely focus on someone else's weaknesses as a way to feel better about themselves.

Since scapegoating hinders group movement, the leader needs to be alert to its development in a group. To reverse the process, she may comment, "We seem to be blaming Louise for our failure to progress; what is happening here?" or "Mary, you always tell Jerry he is wrong, but is it possible you have some critical feelings toward me, too?"

To deal effectively with scapegoating, the leader must be willing to accept anger. If the source of scapegoating is anger toward the leader, she needs to be able to accept verbal anger, resentment, or disappointment without trying to change the subject, to comply with unrealistic group demands, or to retaliate in subtle ways. By accepting group anger appropriately, the leader can help the group to learn that authority figures are human and should not be expected to meet everyone's needs, but that this does not necessarily mean that they are punitive or non-accepting of others' feelings.

SILENCE

The ability to use silence effectively is a learned skill. Some silences are useful to group movement, others are not. Silence can be a group or an individual phenomenon. In either case, silence can have a number of meanings. Individual silence may mean that the person is holding back information or self in order to punish the group or the leader, that he may fear displeasing others, that he is in agreement, or that he is trying to escape talking because he is anxious.

When silence pervades the group early, it is often used to conceal that group members are anxious and unsure of what to do. Those who are least comfortable with silence will usually speak first. Often those who break silences do so because they think they are responsible for keeping the group moving. Sad silences may follow discussion of separation, death, or ending of the group. Angry silences follow angry interchanges and may be clues to hidden hostility or resentment that can decrease group movement. Finally, thoughtful silences can occur after an especially relevant interchange.

In many groups there is a tendency to assume that the leader should break silences, and this may be most comfortable for an inexperienced leader. In general, it is best for the leader not to break silences unless they appear to be building into a power struggle over who will speak first. In this case, the leader might comment, "What's all the silence about?" Thoughtful silences help group movement and should not be broken by the leader. Likewise, anxious silences should not be broken by the leader unless tension levels seem to be highly disturbing to group members. Sad silences allow the group to grieve, reminisce, or resolve feelings, and they are constructive to group movement.

In teaching or time-limited groups, the leader may have to decide whether it is more important to break the silence in order to convey information, or whether the group could profit from being silent. Whenever the leader does break a silence, it should not be done to introduce a new topic, but rather to focus the group's thinking on the meaning of the silence or what happened prior to it. A leader who breaks silences frequently needs to examine why she feels she must always be the one to keep the group moving. She might helpfully comment, after a silence, "Silence sometimes makes people uncomfortable; does anyone have any ideas why this is so?" or "What are you thinking?" or "We have a couple of people here who aren't talking. Does anyone have any thoughts about this?"

NEW MEMBERS

Highly cohesive groups will have a stronger reaction to a new group member than those that are less cohesive. Regardless of the level of cohesiveness, group members frequently have mixed feelings about the prospect of receiving a new member into the group; they may hope that the new person will contribute positively to group goals, but they may also be worried that he will upset old patterns of interaction or compete for power or leadership. The new member will also probably have mixed feelings about joining the group; he may wonder whether he will be accepted or rejected, and whether this will be a satisfying or a threatening experience.

Whenever a new member is to be added to a group, the leader can help him to be more sure of himself by meeting him individually before he attends the first session. This gives her an opportunity to explain the group goal, to state any standing rules for group behavior, and to tell the person when and where the group will meet and for how long. She should encourage the new member to ask questions and to share his expectations concerning the group experience.

The group should also be prepared for the change in membership. The leader can ask the group for reactions to adding a new member. This tactic might enable her to reduce the potential for hostility or rejection of the new member. It would also be helpful to ask members to introduce themselves to the newcomer and to tell a little about who they are and what has transpired so far in the group.

Close observation of the group on the day the new member enters it can help the leader to determine whether intervention is necessary. If she notes that tension levels rise, she can try to put the new member at ease by turning to him with a comment such as "You'll soon catch on to what happens." If the group is hostile or rejecting of the new member, she can intervene by saying, "I guess the group is upset about having a new member. Let's take some time to talk about this." However, overdisclosure can occur when a new member is anxious and uses talk about himself to decrease anxiety; the leader must guard against this. Such behavior can break group norms and frighten or increase tension levels in members who have been part of the group for a longer time. The new member might also react negatively after the session and even decide not to return. For these reasons, the leader will find it helpful to redirect group interaction by asking other members to express their thoughts or feelings.

TRANSFERENCE AND
COUNTERTRANSFERENCE

Group members tend to project aspects of former relationships onto current figures in the group setting. This transfer of feelings that were initially evoked by parents or other significant people in a person's life is called transference. Transference occurs when a group member reacts toward the leader as he did toward a parent, since he identifies both as authority figures. If the person's parent was harsh and unloving, he will probably expect the group leader to be the same and tend to discount leader behavior that is warm and loving. Or the leader may remind a group member of an aunt to whom she has been very close; this member may be extremely friendly toward the leader—far beyond what would be expected in a brief relationship. When the leader of a group is quiet, those in the group who have had the "silent treatment" from parents or significant others may react toward her with transference of their earlier feelings of resentment. Group members may transfer onto others their feelings of love, hate, competition, or even guilt that they feel (or felt) toward brothers, sisters, husbands, or other family members.

Group members frequently try to duplicate family relationships within the group. Such transference can be the start of real friendship or of arguments; they need to be considered as the distorted relationships that they are. Leaders may feel a strong pull to act out the roles group members try to cast them in; to do so would not be a therapeutic way to relate to the persons involved.

A leader who responds to group members because they evoke reactions reminiscent of her own earlier relationships is engaging in countertransference. This occurs when a group member reminds the leader of past experiences with significant people who had acted similarly and had irritated her, were menacing, showed the need to be cared for, were of a different race or cultural group (and were therefore not completely understood), or, on the other hand, who had qualities that were attractive. Because of these past experiences, the leader is likely to react with anxiety or a sense of immediate recognition when meeting group members who have styles of relating that tap memories of these past relationships. In such cases, the leader is likely to be unreasonably irritated by, fearful or overprotective of, underreactive to, or attracted by one or more group members. The effect on the group is to provoke anxiety and disruption of communication.

The leader needs to be aware of any overreaction to group members; to neglect to do so is bound to lead to anxiety both in herself and the group and will impede group movement. The novice leader might try to deny the existence of countertransference reactions even though they seem to be universal experiences. Rather than trying to hide the existence of such reactions, it would be useful for the leader to remember that countertransference is an expected reaction that frequently occurs when helping people are highly involved with patients or clients.

PHYSICAL AGGRESSION

The leader cannot allow any physically aggressive behavior among group members. This includes touching group members who do not wish to be touched, throwing restricted objects, and hitting or hurting oneself or others. Such behavior must be halted immediately, and firm limits must be set so that all group members will feel safe within the group setting. In many adult groups, the leader will decide before the first session that touching will not be allowed; this rule is often set so that people will be encouraged to express their feelings verbally rather than through potentially dangerous actions. Other leaders will wait until physically aggressive behavior occurs, and then set limits.

For adult groups, a number of interventions is available to the leader. At the first sign of difficulty she can say, "No touching in this group," or "Stop hitting me. I won't allow you to hurt me," or "No throwing; somebody could get hurt." The rationale behind this intervention is that the leader demonstrates respect for self and others by limiting physically destructive behavior. If this technique does not work, the leader can gently but firmly restrain the member. Or she may ask the member to leave the group and return when he is ready to express verbally what he feels. Another tactic is to ask the aggressive member to sit next to the leader; often people who are physically aggressive are frightened. But if the leader is very frightened herself, this intervention probably would not accomplish anything. Another way of intervening might be to say, "Tell us in words what you're feeling." The leader might also ask group members what they think and how they feel about their fellow member's behavior. This can evoke strong reactions as members recall past situations in which similar behavior occurred and can lead to fruitful discussions. When all else fails, and if the leader feels comfortable doing so, she can share her feelings with the physically aggressive person. She might say, "I want to help you, but I can't do much about it when I'm frightened and can't use my energy trying to be helpful."

The leader in a children's group can first acknowledge the child's feelings; "You're angry and you want to hit me?" Next, she can clearly state the limit of behavior: "No hitting allowed here." Then she can suggest other channels for releasing anger: "Here, hit this pillow instead of me," or "Tell me in words what you are feeling." Finally, the child can be asked how he feels about being restricted: "What do you think about not being able to hit me?" For younger children, the leader may use nonverbal methods: she may hover over the child in a calm, protective manner, or she may use her own arms or legs to restrain the child's arms or legs gently but firmly. When the child relaxes, he may be able to cry (in relief) and/or talk about his feelings (Pothier, 1976).

NONVERBAL GROUPS OR GROUP MEMBERS

Children or elderly persons may be less able to express their thoughts and feelings verbally in groups than are people of other ages. This does not hold true for all groups, however, since adolescents and young adults or middle-aged persons may also have difficulty expressing themselves verbally. Whenever this is a factor in group conduct, the leader may need to develop techniques for stimulating group interaction. Planning and implementing a group activity such as cooking a meal or taking a trip to a favorite place is one way to get group members involved in different types of interaction with one another.

When the leader is unsure of nonverbal or silent members' reactions to a group session, she can learn about their thoughts, feelings, and perceptions by asking them to write on a card or piece of paper a summary of the main things that have occurred during the session, or to respond to an incomplete sentence. Some stems for nonverbal groups include:

Today, I feel . . . .
Having diabetes means . . . .
Being in this place is . . . .
I wish someone would ask me about . . . .
The worst (best) thing that happened to me since the last
    meeting was . . . .
The thing I remember most about our last meeting was . . .
. . . .
I like (dislike) this group because . . . .

Once the members have completed one of the above incomplete sentences, the leader might collect them, select one or more, and use the information as a focus for discussion. Merely reading them aloud may stimulate discussion. If no one responds verbally, hearing the ideas of others read aloud can be useful and may increase cohesiveness. Before reading anyone's comments aloud, however, it is best to check with the group to make sure that no one minds. Keep members' comments anonymous unless members volunteer that the remark is theirs.

To stimulate group discussion, the leader can also ask group members to draw pictures of themselves or of their families. She may also bring a living or inanimate object to the group to serve as a focus for discussion and nonverbal interaction; she might bring a kitten, a loaf of freshly baked bread, a plant or some flowers, or a picture. Using a picture that contains one or more people, the leader can ask each group member to tell what he thinks the person in the picture is thinking, feeling, or doing; this may initiate discussions about attitudes, biases, and other barriers to working together or communicating with other people.

Movement and structured exercises will help to release tension, build group feeling, and teach control of impulses. One group member may be asked to start a movement, and the rest of the group is asked to imitate it. This process is repeated, until each group member has led and has followed the movements of the others.

Even though group members may be essentially nonverbal in their interactions, the leader can make many observations about the group when activity is their primary focus. She can look for smaller groupings within larger groupings; who plays with whom; who leads and who follows; and for changes in these patternings. Relationship to the leader is another area to be examined—which group members withdraw, battle, ask for help from the leader, challenge others, channel or divert the focus of activity, cry, or laugh. Group members who can express their feelings and thoughts readily will still communicate during activities as one member tries to get another to do what she wants, makes suggestions, threatens others, or carries out the activity. The leader can also learn about the various group members by observing the atmosphere in the group. Is it busy, apathetic, noisy, scattered in activity, aggressive, peaceful? How do members react to support, approval, suggestion, and limit setting from others? What themes of play or work can be identified, and how do they compare with normal growth and development levels for that age group? Finally, what individual styles of relating to the materials or activity can be discerned, and how can these styles be best described—that is, are they scattered, unrelated, concerned with being enclosed or shutting out others, experimental, creative, secretive, attacking, disorganized, stereotyped in thought or action?

ABSENCES

Absences from a scheduled group session may be due to real factors such as car failure or illness, but they can also be due to anxiety and fear about what is happening in the group. Absenteeism may also be related to group size; when many members are involved, subgroups and time limits can prohibit satisfying participation. It can also be a form of testing group limits. The absent member may be indirectly asking "Am I accepted or missed?" In other instances, absence occurs because the group takes low priority in the member's life.

When the group leader assesses the source of absenteeism, she may find that she needs to do something to reduce anxiety. She may poll the group to ascertain goal relevance for the members, create a smaller group, evaluate leadership skills and/or open up the problem of absenteeism for group discussion. In the latter case she may ask, "How do you think it affects the group when everyone's not here?" The leader should also try to contact absent members via phone or letter, not in order to make them feel guilty, but to convey concern. Members need to know that their presence is desired, that they have been missed, and that the leader is concerned about them. In highly cohesive groups, a group member may volunteer to contact an absent member with whom he is friendly.

MANIPULATION

Group members may try to manipulate other group members, including the leader, to meet their own special needs. One member may be especially charming and helpful to the leader in the hope of being recognized as a favored child with special privileges; the leader may fall prey to this kind of seduction and, by rewarding compliant behavior, hope to get the group moving. Another member may try to put someone else on the "hot seat." In both cases, the leader needs to guard against rewarding or punishing the member who attempts to manipulate the group. She can say, "I notice that some of the members seem to be taking advantage of others in the group; has anyone else noticed this?" No names need be called; rather, the topic is introduced to help the group to understand how one member can manipulate the group for his own benefit.

SIMULATED EXERCISES

The two simulated exercises that follow each include an experiential and a discussion section. If the group is large, it should be divided for the simulation into equal-sized groups of not more than 15 members. The entire group can reconvene for the discussion.

Exercise 1

Nonverbal Communication

This exercise is designed to give the nurse leader practical experience in observing and using nonverbal communication modes. Gestures, facial expression, eye contact, body movements, touch, physical distance and proximity, posture, clothes and their arrangement, sign language, silence, vocal and body sounds, and objects all can be used to convey an array of messages to others. Nonverbal communication can be as influential as verbal communication. When nonverbal communication contradicts verbal language, a mixed message results, which is confusing to the observer. For this reason, the nurse who wishes to be an effective leader needs to be aware of her own body language as well as that of other group members. Because this exercise allows participants to focus on nonverbal messages only, it encourages a deeper understanding of an aspect of communication that is often not examined in real-life work, supportive, and teaching groups.

Objectives

1. To practice conveying common feelings without the use of words.

2. To receive feedback regarding nonverbal communication ability.

3. To learn to teach others to be more effective in expressing themselves nonverbally.

Procedure

1. The group or the instructor appoints a timekeeper, who is instructed to make sure that time limits for each section are observed. The timekeeper is directed to warn the group when ten minutes remain to complete the task.

2. A leader is chosen by the group or the instructor for each subgroup.

15-45 minutes

3. The leader asks each person in the group to portray the following feelings, using only nonverbal communication:
   a. tension
   b. anger
   c. love
   d. acceptance
   e. fear

4. The leader intervenes only when a group member is having difficulty expressing the feeling. In that case, the leader asks the group, "What can you tell her to help her show the feeling more clearly?"

The leader coaches the group to help each one express nonverbal messages. The group can be told to draw from experiences in charades, drama, dance, or film. Feelings should be expressed one by one, with time for feedback from group members concerning what is effective and ineffective in the member's presentation of feeling.

5. The leader asks the entire group to discuss the following points:

15-30
minutes

a. What is difficult about using nonverbal communication exclusively?

b. Which nonverbal mode does each member feel most comfortable using, and why?

c. What ideas does the group have about the reason for some modes of communication being used more frequently than others? How could more modes be used by each person?

d. What was learned from this exercise that can be applied in other group situations?

Exercise 2

Stating the Purpose

This exercise gives participants skill in formulating, verbalizing, and assessing others' presentations of group purposes or goals. By formulating and actually putting into words the purpose of the group within which the nurse will be working, goal clarification can be increased, and hesitancy in presenting the group purpose to the real-life group can be decreased.

Objectives

1. To practice stating group purposes or goals to a group.

2. To assess strengths and weaknesses of group purpose presentations.

3. To list important points to be considered when stating a group purpose.

Procedure

1. The group or the instructor appoints a timekeeper, who makes sure that the time limits for each section are observed.

2. The group or the instructor appoints a leader for each subgroup.

3. The leader appoints a recorder to jot down important points to consider when stating a group purpose or goal.

4. The leader asks each member in turn to state the group purpose for the group she is to lead (or be a participant in), as if she were the actual group leader speaking to the group. If some or all participants do not know the purpose of the group or even the group to which they will belong, the following hypothetical groups can be assigned: a teaching group for postoperative patients, a family of a patient who will return home after a long hospitalization, a supportive group for severely burned patients, a consciousness-raising group for men, a supportive group for people with epilepsy, a teaching group for new parents, a nutrition group for prison inmates, a teaching group for patients with congestive heart failure, an orientation group for new nursing staff members, a supportive group for families whose children are dying, a supportive group for people with quadriplegia, a play group for preschoolers, an activity group for senior citizens, a social group for nursing-home residents, an exercise group for psychiatric patients.

5. When each group member has stated her purpose, each of the other group members points out at least one thing that was good about the way the person stated the purpose and one thing that could be improved; then that group member restates the purpose, using the group's suggestions for improvement.

6. The whole group convenes for 15 to 30 minutes to list important points to consider when stating a group purpose.

READINGS

Andrews, Miriam. "Poetry Programs in Mental Hospitals," *Perspectives in Psychiatric Care* 8(1975): 17-18.

Bell, Ruth. "Activity as a Tool in Group Therapy," *Perspectives in Psychiatric Care* 8(1070): 84-91.

Clark, Carolyn. "Nonverbal Communication," in *Nursing Concepts and Processes*. Albany, N.Y.: Delmar, 1977.

"Consultation to Groups in Conflict," *Journal of Psychiatric Nursing* 13(1975): 11-15.

Crosson, Carrie. "Art Therapy with Geriatric Patients: Problems of Spontaneity," *American Journal of Art Therapy* 15(1976): 51-56.

Dinkmeyer, Don, and James Muro. "Special Problems in Groups," in *Group Counseling*. Itasca, Ill.: F.E. Peacock, 1971.

Eisenberg, Joann, and Ruth Abbott. "The Monopolizing Patient in Group Therapy," *Perspectives in Psychiatric Care* 6(1968): 92-93.

Fox, Madeleine. "Talking with Patients Who Can't Answer," *American Journal of Nursing* 71(1971): 1146.

Gosciewski, William. "Photo Counseling," *Personnel and Guidance Journal* 53(1975): 600-604.

Hall, Edward. *The Silent Language*. Garden City, N.Y.: Doubleday, 1973.

Pothier, Patricia. *Mental Health Counseling with Children*. Boston: Little, Brown, 1976.

Rubin, Judith. "Through Art to Affect: Blind Children Express Their Feelings," *New Outlook for the Blind* 69(1975): 385-391.

Schwartz, Lawrence, and Jane Schwartz. "Transference: The Hidden Element in Your Relations with Patients," *Nursing '73* 3(1973): 37-41.

Vidoni, Clotilde. "Development of Intense Countertransference Feelings in the Therapist toward a Patient," *American Journal of Nursing* 75(1975): 407-409.

Whitaker, Dorothy. "Some Conditions for Effective Work with Groups," *British Journal of Social Work* 5(1975): 423-439.

White, Eleanor. "Group Psychotherapy," in *New Dimensions in Mental Health Psychiatric Nursing*, edited by Marion Kalkman and Anne Davis. New York: McGraw-Hill, 1974.

Zeiger, Betty. "Life Review in Art Therapy with the Aged," *American Journal of Art Therapy* 15(1976): 47-50.

4

Beginning, Guiding, and Terminating the Group

PREMEETING PREPARATION

Much of the preparation needed should be done by the nurse group leader before the first group meeting. Three major preparatory tasks for the group leader are (1) handling administrative details and relationships: (2) making structural decisions about the group; and (3) interviewing or notifying prospective group members.

Administrative Issues

The novice group leader may think that the patient or work group will be the largest system with which she will need to be concerned. In reality, group members will be greatly influenced by other systems such as family, community agency, hospital, and other institutional systems. Therefore, the nurse leader who expects to provide a group experience for patients or clients must consider how (and whether) these various systems interrelate. Highly organized bureaucratic institutions such as prisons, long-term hospitals, and even schools may present the greatest resistance to innovative suggestions by a nurse who suggests that she lead a group within their walls. The nurse's first task in such a setting may be simply to locate the appropriate administrator who can grant access to a group population. It is important to note that although highly organized institutions may present the most resistance to the nurse as group leader, smaller community agencies can also be resistant to change.

The nurse may have to educate administrators about how nurses can function as group leaders in task, supportive, and teaching groups. Since nurse-led groups are a relatively new development in some settings, considerable restatement and reinforcement may be needed regarding just how the nurse can function in this role. The nurse leader should expect to spend a great deal of time and effort working through system resistance prior to and while leading a group of patients or clients.

Resistance may be decreased if the leader can clearly spell out objectives for the group experience and potential group content during planning sessions. The clearer she can be about her expectations and plans, the less likelihood there will be later that administrators may directly or indirectly undermine group movement. Group experiences should be presented as a joint venture, and it is especially important for the leader to help administrators to specify their expectations of how she will function. Points that need to be agreed upon include deciding on whether administrators will receive feedback about group functioning and exactly how this will be done; deciding who will be involved in the mechanics of setting the time, length, and place for group meetings; and deciding who will enlist, convene, and retrieve group members, and how this will be accomplished.

In summary, the leader who is about to start a new group needs to consider the following factors:

1. the larger systems within which the group population exists;
2. the appropriate administrator or authority figure who can give permission for the group to begin;

3. the administrator's knowledge regarding how a nurse functions as a group leader;
4. an appropriate way to communicate the leader's expectations and plans for a group experience, including objectives or goals and a potential agenda or list of possible topics to be discussed;
5. the administrator's expectations about the group experience;
6. how to collaborate with the administrator in deciding how information will be shared once the group starts;
7. ways to agree on a method to ensure smooth handling of the mechanics of group operation.

Decisions about the Group

The first decision to be made by the group leader is the makeup of the group to be led. In some cases this will be determined by the needs and availability of patient or staff populations, or by the nurse's job description or assignment. In other situations, the leader may have developed an interest in a certain problem area and may wish to lead a group of other interested people. If, for example, the nurse is interested in patients' emotional reactions to the physical illness process, she may decide to start a group for people—either patients or families of patients—who are involved with such illnesses. At some point, the leader will have to decide whether the group is to consist of people with acute or chronic illness, or with only one certain illness, and whether it should be limited to patients of a certain age; she must also decide whether to include family members or friends who might be involved in the patient's care. Yet another point for the leader to think about is the way potential group members may relate to each other. If the leader suspects that most of the candidates will be withdrawn and monosyllabic, she knows she will have a more difficult time in stimulating group interaction; if she decides to add several members who are likely to be more verbal, she runs the risk of having these members dominate the group.

One guideline for deciding on group membership is that close friends and relatives should probably not be included in the same group, since they may tend to reinforce old behavioral patterns. All members of children's groups should be of the same developmental level; when exercise or skill is the focus of the group, the children should be of approximately the same ability so as to eliminate feelings of failure or the scapegoating of less skilled members.

At times, the leader will have few options as to choice of members. Perhaps only six or eight people who meet the requirements of the group will be available. If the group is to be made-up of nursing aides, membership will be predetermined by the number of available aides on the unit. An inservice educator who plans to lead an orientation group for nurses may find that the group membership will be determined largely by decisions made in the personnel and nursing offices.

Regardless of how group membership is determined, the leader needs to consider the aspect of group size. Groups of four to twelve members are the optimal size when frequent interaction and group cohesiveness are objectives. When the leader is inexperienced, or when children or highly verbal or active adults compose the group, it may be advisable to limit groups to four to five members. Groups of six or seven, or even more, can be formed when there is more than one group leader, when group members are primarily nonverbal, when the leader is more experienced, or when structured exercises or learning situations are used. The leader should remember that as groups become larger, the potential for cohesiveness decreases since there is less opportunity for members to interact with one another.

The leader also makes the important decision regarding how often the group should meet. Again, more frequent meetings are likely to lead to greater cohesiveness. In a busy hospital unit, however, meeting more than once a week or once every other week may become a problem in terms of scheduling.

The decision about the length of group meetings is dependent on several factors—the leader's time and energy level, the group's attention level, the purpose of the group, and the group's need for a warming-up period. Novice group leaders may feel quite drained physically after a 40-minute session because they are not yet skilled enough to cope with the highly complex and stimulating atmosphere of group interaction. For these leaders, it would seem wise to limit group sessions to 40 minutes until the leader has developed the skill and supervisory abilities needed to deal with longer sessions. Children's groups may also meet for less than an hour, depending on the members' attention span. Some groups seem to require a warming-up period of 10 to 15 minutes for chatting and socializing before work starts. This may be a useful device, and the leader may need to decide whether the meeting time should be expanded to an hour and a half so that more work toward the group goal could be accomplished. Once a time limit is set, however, it should not be changed whimsically or without discussion of the pros and cons with both the supervisor and the group members. This is important for several reasons. First, by structuring the group and keeping the time and frequency of meetings the same, the leader maintains a consistency, which, over time, can demonstrate to the group that she is trustworthy, responsible, and able to stick to limits. Second, short-term groups are likely to accomplish more if they know the time limits of their existence. Groups in which the prevailing philosophy is "This group will go on forever, so why rush into anything?" will accomplish little. The leader who runs a short-term group can encourage more efficient movement toward the group goal by stating at the beginning and end of each meeting, "We have x meetings left to accomplish the goal." Lastly, a consistent time structure is important if members tend to try to make it necessary for the group leader to extend a session by bringing up an important issue at the end of the time allotted; in these cases, it is better not to extend the session, because it teaches the group to work within limits without waiting until the last moment to bring up important matters. To assist in this teaching effort, the leader can remind the group at intervals, "We have 30 minutes left today" or "We have ten minutes left for talking today."

The total number of group sessions may be predetermined by the agency or the availability of group members. Groups that continually take on new members and lose old ones, such as orientation groups in professional agencies, or about-to-be-discharged patient groups, may be ongoing. Planning or supportive groups, on the other hand, may be circumscribed and only exist until group goals can be attained.

Whether groups are ongoing or not, the leader must decide whether they will be open or closed. Open groups are those to which new members may be added. When the open group system is used, the leader needs to identify a population pool from which to draw additional group members. Closed groups are those that do not add new members, despite the fact that some may leave the group before it officially terminates. Neither is the better system, but deciding on this point is another matter for the leader to weigh and evaluate. In doing this evaluation, the leader may consider whether the potential population is large enough to support an open group; how and when this potential population could be oriented about possible group membership; whether introducing new members would slow movement of the group toward its goal; and whether the group could exist and work with only two or three members.

Group sessions should always be held in the same place, if possible. The meeting-room should be private, uncluttered, well ventilated, have comfortable seating arrangements (preferably circular to encourage interaction), and be readily accessible in terms of transportation. The leader will have to decide whether smoking will be permitted. When health concerns are being discussed, she will also need to consider whether her own smoking (and/or allowing others to smoke) provides a useful role model of healthful behavior. Likewise, furnishing high-calorie, low-nutrition foods such as cookies and ice cream to poorly nourished group members is a consideration to be balanced off against the reward factor of offering sweets as an inducement to participate. Such a trade-off may be more easily resolved if the leader decides to offer fruit juice and a nut-and-fruit bread or some other sweet but nutritive combination.

No group leader can force group members to attend the group meetings. (However, in some institutional settings, staff members often bring people to meetings in wheelchairs or make special privileges contingent upon group attendance.) About the most the leader can do is to stress the idea that a group experience has potential usefulness and that for the group to be of the most benefit to all the members, all sessions should be attended by the complete membership.

The goals or objectives that the leader formulates for the group experience depend on the type of group and its duration and the agency constraints. Some agencies become quite involved and influential in constructing group goals; others leave this task almost entirely up to the leader. For some groups, the leader's purpose may be to help clients to formulate their own goals. Group goals are best stated in behavioral terms using action verbs that connote observable behaviors. When goals are stated in this way, both leader and group members know when goals have been attained. Some group goals that have been stated in behavioral terms include:

> to role play job interviews;
> to practice colostomy irrigation;
> to prepare an ethnic meal;
> to state four purposes of breast feeding;
> to plan health care for patients on Unit 6C:
> to practice three alternative ways to express anger;
> to demonstrate effective breathing techniques for each stage
>   of labor;
> to share thoughts and feelings about having diabetes;
> to develop alternative ways to handle other people's reac-
>   tions to disability.

When choosing a probable group goal, the leader considers how to state the goal in clear terms, and she specifies the tasks that must be performed to accomplish the goal and some interaction processes that probably will occur or be encouraged among group members. Most groups have a number of goals; some are short-term goals, others are medium- or long-term. The importance of specifying goals is that they guide group action and motivate members to work in a specific direction. Some variables that can affect whether groups meet their goals are: (1) the extent to which goals are defined in clear, observable behaviors; (2) whether members see the goals as meaningful; (3) a cooperative group atmosphere; (4) consistency between individual and group goals; (5) small risk of failure; (6) availability of resources to meet goals; and (7) the allowance of enough time and flexibility to modify and attain goals.

Preparing Prospective Group Members

When selecting a group of patients or clients for a group, it is best for the leader to interview each potential member individually. This interview may be either brief or extensive, depending on the purpose of the group. The leader may conduct more extensive interviews if she is concerned about balancing the composition of the group, or if the group experience needs to be explained fully to the prospective member. For example, prospective members of a supportive group for cancer patients may need time to learn more about the proposed experience and to react to the idea of being in a discussion group with others who have the same condition.

A short lecture or summary of learning content can be given to patients who are being considered for a teaching group. Written or recorded materials can also be used to give potential group members a better idea of what to expect.

Factual information about how the group will operate is given to prospective members before the first meeting of the group. "Group contract" is the term used to refer to the basic operating agreement between leader and group members (see Figure 2). This contract can be either written or verbal; either way, it is intended as a statement of group structure and expected group behavior. Statements in the contract cover such data as number of sessions; time and frequency of meetings; whether the group will accept new members if some leave; member and leader responsibilities for confidentiality; how recording equipment will be used by the leader; limits of behavior such as attendance and physical aggression; specific expectations about participation, goals, and (if applicable) fees. The contract can provide

Figure 2
Written Group Contract

I agree to attend ten sessions with a group of other new parents to learn parenting skills. I realize that the group will meet every Monday evening from 7 p.m. to 8 p.m. and that I will be expected to attend each meeting at the University Center. I know that anecdotes of individual parents are confidential, and not to be shared outside the group. I understand that a nursing student will record what is said in the group as part of a learning experience in group dynamics, but that the recordings will only be shared with her instructor for learning purposes.

....
Group member's signature and date

....
Leader's signature and date

---

both structure and safety for group members. People frequently enter a group with many misconceptions about what will happen during the sessions. The more time the leader spends discussing the contract before the first meeting, the better the chances that a climate of collaboration will be created. The leader should avoid presenting too much information regarding the contract in a short period of time, because prospective members who are highly anxious may distort or selectively fail to hear specific aspects of what is being said. No matter how detailed or how general the group contract, it is wise to give members an opportunity to express their ideas and feelings about the items. While preparing group members, the leader also encourages each one to state what he or she hopes to learn from the group experience or how each hopes to benefit from it.

The group contract may not necessarily be used for a working or task group. However, it is useful to invite reactions and, if possible, to orient prospective members to the group goals, frequency, and duration of meetings, and to limits and expectations for member behavior within the group.

EARLY GROUP MEETINGS

During the first meeting of a group, it often becomes apparent that individual members have some goals that are at cross-purposes to the group goals. These individual goals are referred to as hidden agendas. Leaders, too, may have hidden agendas. For example, the leader may say it is up to the group to decide what its goals are, although she has already decided on the direction in which she thinks the group should go. Or the group goal may be to share thoughts and feelings about having cancer, but one of the individual members may hope that he will be cured in the group. Hidden agendas in supportive or therapeutic groups often reflect the expectation that the leader will provide special safety, protection, advice, or knowledge. Whatever the items on the hidden agenda, they can be detrimental to effective group work, and the leader needs to act to decrease this potential. During the first meeting of the group, she should restate the agreed-upon goal and give the group a chance to discuss it thoroughly in order to clarify misunderstandings any of the members may have about how to reach the goal. Hidden agendas that are unrealistic and discordant with group goals need to be examined by the whole group. The leader may say, "I wonder if we've said everything about this goal? Perhaps we could go around the group so everyone can have a chance to add his particular thoughts and feelings about it." Although it may seem that undue stress is being placed on this point, novice group leaders can often trace later group problems to insufficient clarification of the group goal.

Once the goal has been clarified, the leader might restate it for emphasis. She might say to a supportive group for children with diabetes, "This group is for kids with diabetes to share with one another experiences they have had with others who do not have diabetes." In addition, the leader might start the group off by having them tell, in turn, what it was like when they found out they had diabetes.

Especially in supportive groups, but also in task and teaching groups, the ambiguity of the situation often causes a certain amount of anxiety. Therefore, members will use their usual means of coping with anxiety. Some will attempt to seek structure and reassurance by demonstrating dependency on the leader or on other group members; to prompt the leader to care for them, they will ask many questions, seek advice, or behave ineptly. Others may pair off to provide mutual support; this phenomenon is referred to as pairing. Still others may deal with their anxiety by acting as assistant leader or teacher.

The communication in early group sessions is often stereotyped, intellectual, and rational, following norms for usual social conversation. This early communication structure allows members to get to know one another slowly; too high (as well as too low) levels of self-disclosure inhibit early group movement. Some common themes in early group meetings are trust, safety, and dependency.

Although the group leader attempts to create a climate of acceptance and comfort, she also tries to stay away from the role of the all-knowing, all-giving parent or "expert." Group members will repeatedly try to cast the leader in that role. The leader needs to see this as a form of dependency. When she persistently refuses to be the "authority," group members will probably become angry. Some anger, directed at the leader, is an expected part of the group process and needs to occur in order to enable high-level cohesiveness and relatedness to emerge. If anger is not expressed directly ("You're the leader, do something!"), it will often emerge indirectly ("The staff here is not doing their job," or "The staff mistreats us"). This particular form of attack often startles the novice leader, who may jump in to defend herself or others or try to be the ultimate authority. Neither of these responses is particularly helpful. Instead, the leader can use her reactions of frustration, anger, anxiety, or guilt to "hear" and understand what is going on in the group. In supportive groups, the leader may do more than just understand;

she may comment, "I wonder if the group is irritated with me because I don't have all the answers?" By helping the group to understand and verbalize its concerns, the leader helps the group to move toward its goals.

The leader can perform three important functions during early group meetings: (1) develop a sense of cohesion and connectedness in the group; (2) provide sufficient structure for group interaction in order to keep anxiety at a tolerable level; and (3), identify the basic norms for group behavior. It is to be expected that group members will talk to the group leader more often than they talk to one another. Very early in group sessions, the leader can begin to promote interaction and connectedness by assisting members to talk to one another; she might say, "I don't know. Who in the group has a thought about that?" or "Ask Jimmy that one," or "Tell Mrs. Lane what you just told me." In teaching or activity groups, the leader can promote group interaction by saying, "Show Sarah how to draw up the medication, Andy," or "Toss the ball once to every member in the group; you start, Wayne," or "Perhaps Mr. Edwards can tell us how he handles that problem." By not providing all the answers or doing all the tasks, the leader gives the message that the members are capable of taking some responsibility for what happens in their group.

Another tactic the leader can use to increase group interaction is to reward participation through verbal and nonverbal communication. For example, the leader might say, "You seemed unsure about sharing with us, but you were able to do it!" or "Learning to breathe efficiently in preparation for labor is difficult, but you've made progress today." Nonverbal communications such as head nods and eye contact can be used to reward members when they speak or participate.

In the supportive group, the focus is on encouraging group members to share their thoughts, feelings, and reactions to crises, health conditions, or interpersonal relationships. A discussion or teaching group has a different kind of focus and structure. Since there must be a shared understanding of the language that is to be used, terms and concepts may need to be defined. The leader may ask members to draw up a list of words or concepts they do not fully understand. Part of the session can then be devoted to clarifying the meanings of the words and to checking to see that all members understand the terms.

As in other groups, the goals and objectives for teaching and discussion groups should be clearly stated. Since there may be new goals for each session, the leader should state the goal at the beginning of each meeting. Time should be set aside for discussion of each topic or agenda item. The leader may appoint a timekeeper to see that sufficient time is spent on each topic. The group is encouraged to help decide the priority of items to be discussed. The leader can help members to integrate new information by relating material to previous topics, by comparing and contrasting new and old information, and by summarizing and reviewing. Time needs to be allowed for application of new learnings or decisions. Depending on the type of group, members can be asked to identify the implications of the day's session for their lives, work, and/or their relationships with others. At the end of a session, group members can be asked to tell how or whether the session has been useful and to suggest topics for the next session.

Regardless of the stated purpose of the group, the leader tries to encourage members to share their common problems or interests. One of the major benefits of any group experience is learning that others are struggling with the same difficulties or decisions. The leader can point out common issues or problems and suggest that "these are important things for us to discuss at some point." In beginning groups, the members may not be ready to discuss the issues, but by merely indicating their importance, the leader opens the door for discussion at a later date.

GUIDING THE GROUP

As the group progresses, the leader continues to be a role model for clear, effective communication (see Chapter 2). She is adept at revising goals as work progresses or as circumstances within the group change. She begins to teach group members to share leadership. By summarizing what occurs in the group sessions, the leader teaches group members how to organize group experiences in a meaningful way; for example: "Today we've covered how to sterilize syringes," and "We're moving closer to a decision," and "I wonder if we haven't been talking about feeling angry because several members have left the group." As the group begins to take more responsibility, the leader can ask one member to summarize what happened in a particular session. The leader also teaches the group how to clarify thoughts and feelings; she might comment, "Tommy, you seem to be expressing anger; am I right?" or "I think you're both making the same point about disliking overtalkativeness."

The group can also be taught to solve problems, using clarification of the problem as the first step. "The problem seems to be that we need to decide on a topic for next week," or "Barry could use some help from the group in drawing up the medication." Once the problem has been clarified, the leader can ask the members to volunteer their ideas about how to solve the problem and then guide them in testing out or thinking through the possible results of each solution suggested.

A few noisy group members can prevent the group from reaching its goals. In a supportive group, the leader might ask the others to deal with the problem by saying, "Jack and Franny are forming their own group; what do you think is happening there?" In a teaching group, she might ask the noisy members to demonstrate a procedure or give their suggestions about the topic being discussed. In a group of elderly patients, the leader needs to assess whether the noisy pair is temporarily disoriented; if this is the case, the leader might ask them to try to listen to what is being said, or she may provide them with written or verbal orientation to the focus of the group's interaction at that moment.

As the group begins to move into the working phase, members feel concern about their position in relation to the leader and other group members. Also, there is less need for control, so that members' behavior in the group is socially acceptable; this is evidenced by the use of slang, swearing, and informality, and the ability to deal with more complex issues. Depending on the type of group, the leader will observe other signs that the working phase has been entered. Often, members become more involved in sharing and intimacy issues; they seem to be testing out how much they want to reveal about themselves and how close they wish to be to others. Cohesiveness increases, along with a sense of respect and acceptance of self and others, and there is more sharing of personal data and reactions to others in the group. In testing to find the limits of interdependency, independent group members may engage in conflict with one another or in direct or indirect war with the leader. It is important that the leader does not take sides or make judgments about who is right or who started an argument. Also, the leader must be vigilant about not giving in to her own tendency to retaliate when group members challenge her authority. Although at this stage there appears to be a definite shift in behavior, some of the behaviors typical of the working phase may appear in early group meetings (see Figure 3).

Figure 3
Early and Later Group Behaviors

Orientation Phase	Working Phase
Dependency on the leader	Interdependency and shared leadership
Anger that the leader is not omniscient or omnipotent	Increased intimacy and sharing
Attempts to play assistant leader	Conflict between members and/or with the leader
Stereotyped, intellectual-rational and socially acceptable conversation	Conversation on a deeper, less superficial level
Learning about others' similarities	Increased sense of respect and acceptance of other group members
Refining group goals	Collaborative effort in identifying and dealing with group issues

Figure 4
Some Effective Leader Behaviors

Techniques	Examples
Reflection	"You feel . . . ?
Deflection	"What do group members think about that?"
Clarification	"I wonder if you're asking the group for assistance, Mrs. Tanner?"
Asking for group reaction	"How do group members feel about not meeting last week?"
Increasing cohesiveness	"Many of you seem to be expressing an interest in changing the group goal."
Promoting interaction	"I don't know; ask Tom."
Exploring	"Tell us more about that."
Teaching decision making	"As I see it, the problem is to decide on an activity; let's pool our ideas. Who will start?"
Summarizing	"So far we've talked about sterilizing equipment, but not about drawing up medication."

Figure 4 shows leader behaviors that can be effective in moving the group from the orientation to the working phase.

TERMINATING THE GROUP

The process of terminating a group is both a group and an individual task. The entire group may disband, or several members may leave the group at one time. When termination is handled effectively, members can learn how to deal with the separation from others that occurs in many life situations. The ability to say goodbye and move on to other relationships is a skill some people have never learned.

Early in group experiences it is not unusual for members to drop out, because they feel they do not fit in with the group, their expectations are not met, they have been scapegoated by others, they fear success or intimacy, or they have become part of a subgroup that decides to leave. Generally, the leader can make leaving most therapeutic by making goodbyes explicit; for example, by asking, "John is leaving the group; how do you feel about this?" When this is done, there is less chance for unfinished business concerning leave-taking and separation. Especially in supportive groups, it is important for the leader to help the leaving member and the group examine the meaning of separation. Increased understanding can reduce the possibility that both those who leave and those who are left will feel they have failed or been rejected. Instead, the leaving of individual members can be explained as being due to unfitness, poor timing, external pressures, or unreadiness for a group experience. When group members leave a group because they have benefited from and grown through the experience, the termination is less abrupt and can be dealt with in several sessions of the group.

Even when handled well, termination can be anxiety-provoking when it evokes unresolved feelings about previous separations. Some people find it easier to leave the group; others are more comfortable when they are the ones being left. Hopefully, a group experience can help members to be comfortable both with leaving and with being left. Feelings that commonly occur in all types of groups when they end or when group members leave include sadness, anger, rejection, longing, relief, and accomplishment.

In some termination situations, members may attempt to continue the group experience by bringing up new problems or crises for discussion. However, setting new goals or starting new activities when termination is near is not a useful procedure. Rather, the leader can say something like, "This is our last session, and we can't begin to deal with such a complex problem now; we can make better use of our time by discussing our thoughts and feelings about the group experience we have shared." The leader may also wish to continue the group; in that case, she should examine her reluctance to separate.

Termination can be used by the group as a time for review,

just as the end of each session can be thought of as a mini-termination when thoughts, feelings, and accomplishments are summarized. Group members may also use these times to get in touch with unresolved feelings connected with past separations. They may find it difficult to share these feelings, but they should have an opportunity to do so. The leader can take the initiative by sharing her own reflections on the ending or separation and by reviewing the group experience from her point of reference. This may give the group encouragement to share their own reactions. Some group leaders ask for written evaluations or summaries from group members. Whatever method is used, it is the leader's responsibility to provide direction for the group about the way to end a group experience. It is also the leader's responsibility to explore her own reactions to the ending of a group or the leave-taking of group members; once she identifies these feelings, there is less likelihood that she will over- or underreact to terminations.

SIMULATED EXERCISES

Each of the two simulated exercises that follow simulates one session of an actual group meeting. A list of questions to be discussed following completion of the exercises can be used to tie theory to practice. Group members may wish to record on tape either or both simulations and play back the recording to help them answer the discussion questions. If the exercises are completed without an instructor or supervisor present, a later discussion session should be held with a more experienced group leader present.

Each participant should have a copy of this book, if possible, or one or more books can be passed around to enable each person to read the designated material.

Exercise 1
A Simulated Supportive Group
for Cancer Patients and Their Families

This intermediate- to advanced-skill exercise is designed to give the nurse a group experience that simulates some group processes that might occur during one supportive group session. In this simulation, group members role-play communication skills, leadership, anger, dependency, monopolizing, silence, new members, helplessness/hopelessness, and denial. The person who is the designated leader will have practice in leading this simulated group. The other participants will be able to assess how the designated leader led, how this may compare or contrast with their own group leader experiences, how it might feel to be in this type of supportive group, and what problems could be anticipated in a real-life supportive group.

Between nine and fourteen members can play in each simulated group. If more than fourteen people are available, divide learners into groups of between nine and fourteen and begin a new simulation.

Objectives

1. To provide skill practice as leader of a supportive group for one or more participants.

2. To assess communication skills, leadership, anger, dependency, monopolizing, silence, the entrance of a new member, helplessness/hopelessness, and denial as they might occur in a real-life supportive group.

3. To examine alternative ways of dealing with typical group processes.

Procedure

1. Seat the group members in a circle.

2. The group appoints a timekeeper, who times the experiential supportive group to run for 20 minutes and the post-meeting discussion group to run for no more than two hours (the group should spend no more than 15 minutes on each discussion question). The timekeeper may also be assigned to run the tape recorder and/or take notes, depending on the group's decision.

3. The group or instructor appoints a leader for each group of nine to fourteen members. The leader takes the leader role in the simulation (page 80), appoints or asks for volunteers to play the following roles, and assigns each to read her role description only on the indicated pages in this book:
a. dependency role (1-2 players), page 81;

b. overtalkative role (1 player), page 80;
c. denial role (1-2 players), page 80;
d. silent role (1-2 players), page 80;
e. new member role (1 player), page 80;
f. anger role (1-2 players), page 80;
g. helplessness/hopelessness role (1-2 players) page 80.

20 minutes

4. When group members have read their role descriptions on the designated pages, the leader starts the group by saying, "Perhaps each person could tell why they joined this group. Who would like to begin?" The group simulation then continues for 20 minutes.

5. When the timekeeper calls time, the leader or a volunteer from the group leads a group discussion about each of the behaviors enacted, focusing it on the following points:

15 minutes maximum

a. How did the role leader deal with the person who played the denial role? Was it effective? How else could the leader have handled the situation?

15 minutes maximum

b. How did the role leader deal with the person who played the anger role? Was it effective? How else could the leader have handled the situation?

15 minutes maximum

c. How did the role leader deal with the person who played the helplessness/hopelessness role? Was it effective? How else could the leader have handled the situation?

15 minutes maximum

d. How did the role leader deal with the person who played the dependency role? Was it effective? How else could the leader have handled the situation?

15 minutes maximum

e. How did the role leader handle the overtalkative person? Was it effective? How else could the leader have handled the situation?

15 minutes maximum

f. How did the role leader deal with the silent person? Was it effective? How else could the leader have handled the situation?

15 minutes maximum

g. How did the role leader deal with the new member? Was it effective? How else could the leader have handled the situation?

15 minutes or more

h. How did the leader accomplish the four tasks she was assigned?

1. Starting the group: Think of three other ways that could have been used to start this group.

2. Keeping group members talking to one another: Describe comments a group leader might make to encourage interaction among group members.

3. Drawing similarities between group members: Make three statements designed to increase cohesiveness by pointing

out group members' similarities in the simulation in which you have just participated.

4. Ending the group: State one or two other ways to end a group.

Variations: 1. Group members change roles and replay the simulation.

2. Add the roles of personal reactions and dependency, deleting other roles you have already mastered.

Role Descriptions

A SIMULATED SUPPORTIVE GROUP
FOR CANCER PATIENTS AND THEIR FAMILIES

Group Leader Role

Your role has four parts: starting the group action, keeping the members talking to one another instead of you doing all the talking ("Tell the group that" or "Ask if someone else has an aswer for that question"), summarizing what has been said ("Mr. S seems angry, while Mrs. T seems to feel hopeless"), drawing similarities ("Everyone seems to have strong feelings about this"), and terminating the group session ("Our discussion time is up for tonight; see you Thursday night at seven"). Before you begin this simulation, decide whether the group will be composed of patients, families, or a combination of both.

Monopolizing Role

Your role is to continue talking whenever you can. Keep trying to convince the group that you know all about the cause and treatment of cancer.

Denial Role

Your role is to deny the fact that your spouse (or you) is dying of cancer. Whenever anyone in the group starts expressing anger or helplessness, make comments such as, "Don't get so upset," or "Things will get better," or "Cheer up; it's always darkest before the dawn."

Silent Role

Your role is to remain silent throughout this simulation. Observe how the others and especially the leader react to you.

New Member Role

Leave the group before the simulation begins. Come back and join the group in exactly ten minutes.

Anger Role

Your role is to be angry because you (or a family member) are dying from cancer. Whenever you speak, make sure you express irritation. Make comments such as, "How can this happen to me?!" or "How can you sit there so calmly when people are dying?" or "God is punishing me," or "That's a stupid remark."

Helplessness/Hopelessness Role

Your role is to feel helpless and hopeless. Make comments such as, "It's no use; nothing can be done," or "This group can't help me," and "What's the use of talking anyway?"

Variations:

Personal Reactions Role

Imagine someone in your family is dying of cancer. Play the role you think you would play if this occurred.

Dependency Role

Your role is to seek direction from other members in the group, especially the leader. Look at the leader frequently, and make comments such as, "We don't know what this group is for," and "Tell us what to do," or "How can we cope with this problem; it's so overwhelming?"

Exercise 2
A Simulation of a Health Team Meeting

This exercise is designed to give the nurse a group experience that simulates some of the group processes that might occur during one task group session: apathy, conflict, decision making, and leadership. It gives the learner an opportunity to "get the feel" of how these group processes operate by examining and analyzing them in a relatively safe, standardized environment. At least six (and no more than eleven) members act out this simulated exercise or those suggested as variations.

Objectives

1. To allow skill practice as leader of a task group.

2. To practice leadership skills, even though one is not the designated leader.

3. To assess the processes of apathy, conflict, decision making, and leadership as they might occur in an actual task group.

4. To examine alternative ways of dealing with the typical task group processes.

Procedure

1. Seat the group in a circular arrangement.

2. The group appoints a timekeeper, who times the experiential task group to run for 30 minutes and the postsimulation discussion to end after 20 minutes.

3. The group or instructor appoints a leader for each group of six to eleven members who use the simulation. The leader appoints members or asks for volunteers to play the following roles, assigns each to read her role description as presented in this book, and warns each not to read the others' role descriptions:
   a. apathy role (at least two players), page 84;
   b. conflict role (1-2 players), page 84;
   c. decision making role (1-2 players), page 84;
   d. leadership role (1 player; designated by group or leader), page 84.

4. When the group members have read their role descriptions, the leader says, "My role is team leader for this group. We are to plan health care for 50 patients and their families. Since we've not worked together before, we might start out by deciding how we will proceed to develop health care plans for these people. Who has some ideas about how to proceed?"

---

5. The simulation continues until the timekeeper calls time.

6. After time has been called, the leader (or a volunteer from the group) leads the entire group in a discussion of each of the behaviors enacted, focusing on a discussion of each of the following points:

   a. How did the leader deal with the apathetic role players? Was it effective? How else could the leader have handled the situation?

   b. How did the team leader deal with members who displayed conflict? Was it effective? How else could the leader have handled the situation?

   c. How did the leader deal with the group members who tried to assist with decision making? Was it effective? How else could the leader have enlisted their help?

   d. How well did the leader lead? Did others in the group provide leadership functions? List five important leadership functions, and discuss whether they were adequately provided.

   e. Have each participant tell what she learned from this exercise and how it can be applied in other task group situations.

Variations: 1. Group members change roles and replay the simulation.
2. Add the roles of pet project, do-gooder, and/or anticommittee, deleting other roles you have already mastered.

Role Descriptions

A SIMULATION OF A HEALTH TEAM MEETING

Leader Role

Try to fulfill both task and maintenance functions in the group. Try to keep the group moving toward its goal, clarify unclear statements, suggest ways of moving toward the goal, point out movement toward or away from the goal, summarize what others have said, give the group the information it needs to complete its task, and suggest small steps toward the task, such as writing down suggestions given today as a basis for the next meeting's agenda. In fulfilling your maintenance functions, give support to unsure group members, relieve tension, encourage direct communication, voice group feeling, accept group members' ideas, and help the group to evaluate its progress.

Apathy Role

When the simulation begins, yawn frequently, and pretend you are falling asleep. Squirm in your chair, and whisper to other group members. Make frequent suggestions to adjourn the meeting, and refuse to take any responsibility for decision making.

Conflict Role

Express impatience with others' comments. Make derogatory comments, such as "baloney" or "that's a crock." Insist that the group does not know what it is doing or that the group needs an expert to help figure out this planning. Disagree with the team leader whenever you can. Accuse others of not understanding your point of view. Claim that only you know the best way to care for patients and that others are "very poor nurses" and "incompetent practitioners."

Decision Making Role

Try to restate the problem whenever you think others are off the track by saying, "Let's get back to our job," or "You're off the track." If you forget the group goal, ask the team leader to restate it. Clarify or elaborate others' comments with statements such as, "Are you saying that . . . ?" and, "I'd like to add to your idea; what about . . . ." Summarize what has happened every five or ten minutes; for example, make statements such as "Gene has an idea he wants to push, but I'm not sure it's what the rest of us are getting at" or "So far we have decided (or have not decided) to do . . . ." Test to see others' commitment to emerging decisions by saying, "How many agree with the suggestion to . . . . ?"

Variations

Pet Project Role

Imagine you have a pet project, such as consumer advocacy, patients' rights, or preventive health care. Use this team meeting to try to interest others in your pet project. Cite imaginary facts and fallacies related to your pet project. Be sure not to assist the group whose task is to plan health care for the assigned group of patients and families.

Do-Gooder Role

Imagine yourself as a do-gooder, novice nurse leader. Make grandiose plans for health care, without considering restrictions of time, money, or energy.

Anticommittee Role

Imagine you are someone who hates committee meetings and who has had negative experiences while working with other task groups. Tell others about your previous negative experiences rather than focusing on the task at hand.

READINGS

Clark, Carolyn. "Grief Assessment and Intervention," in *Nursing Concepts and Processes.* Albany, N.Y.: Delmar, 1977.

Clark, Carolyn. "Learning to Negotiate the System: A Clinical Experience in Group Dynamics," *Nursing Outlook* 25, 1(1977): 39-42.

Dinkmeyer, Don, and James Muro. *Group Counseling.* Itasca, Ill.: F.E. Peacock, 1971.

Glasser, Paul, Rosemary Sarri, and Robert Vintner, eds. *Individual Change through Small Groups.* New York: Macmillan, 1974.

Gray, Ruth. "Grief," *Nursing '74* 4(1974): 25-27.

Johnson, Don, and Frank Johnson. *Joining Together: Group Theory and Group Skills.* Englewood Cliffs, N.J.: Prentice-Hall, 1975, pp. 87-107.

Marram, Gwen. *The Group Approach in Nursing Practice.* St. Louis, Mo.: C.V. Mosby, 1973.

Pothier, Patricia. *Mental Health Counseling with Children.* Boston: Little, Brown, 1976, pp. 93-102.

Weisman, Avery. *On Dying and Denying.* New York: Behavioral Publications, 1972.

5

Supervision and Coleadership

SUPERVISION

In group work, supervision refers to the interpersonal process whereby leaders present specific data from group sessions to a supervisor, in order to receive feedback about their leadership ability. Supervision of group leaders can occur in a number of different settings and in a variety of ways. Regardless of these variables, the group leader is always entirely responsible for what happens in the group. Although the supervisor can influence the group leader, she cannot be responsible for group process since she is usually not present when the group is led.

Group-work supervision can occur in individual or group settings. The novice group leader may meet individually with a nursing instructor, expert group leader, or fellow student to receive feedback about group leadership skills. This feedback is important because all people have "blind spots" in their perception that can operate to impede group movement, but of which they are unaware. Peers who are no more experienced than the group leader can often provide more objective perceptions because they have not yet been subjected to the pressures and stresses of the group. At the student level, peer supervision involves students supervising one another in their group work, under the guidance of an instructor. By serving as supervisors for one another, they learn not only how to be leaders, but also how to supervise others. Some questions the peer supervisor needs to ask when supervising other group leaders are:

> Did the leader make assumptions without having sufficient data to support them?
> Were theory or concepts regarding observations applied in an appropriate way?
> Were recordings or presentations difficult to understand?
> Were there noticeable gaps in presentation of observations or thoughts?
> Were enough alternative leader actions suggested?
> What evidences were there of transference and counter-transference?
> Was the peer supervisor critical or overbearing with the supervisee?
> Did the peer supervisor create an open, comfortable environment for supervision?
> What needs to be included in an evaluation of the supervisee that the peer supervisor will share with the nursing instructor or supervisor?

Figures 5 and 6 show the results of one hour of peer supervision from both the supervisor's and the supervisee's viewpoint.

Nursing students and graduate students in nursing who lead groups as part of their clinical experience usually receive supervision from nursing faculty. Written or verbal presentations of group process recordings are often used. In some instances, students present videotaped or audiotaped portions of a group session that is being supervised.

In whatever setting supervision occurs, it must focus partly on the supervisory process and on how it relates to group process. It is not unusual for the person being supervised to replicate struggles that are occurring in the group. For example, when the

Figure 5
Group Peer Supervisee Form

Supervisors: *S.C., J.B.*   Supervisees: *C.G., S.T.*

Date of Supervision: *12/11/77*   Type of Group: *Sensory Motor*

Supervision of *3rd group session*   *Stimulation for 5-year-olds*

5 minutes   1.   Problems encountered with this session:

    a. *monopolizing by Teddy*

    b. *Tommy and Sue vie for leader's attention*

    c. *limited attention span of group*

    d. *high anxiety level of leader*

5 minutes   2.   Themes:

    a. *competition,*
      e.g., all trying to be first

    b. *fantasy,*
      e.g., Tommy pretended the toys were real animals

3. Transferences and countertransferences:

    a. *Tommy looked at leader when crying; Susie called him a baby; leader said (protectively), "He is not a baby!" (countertransference)*

    b. *leader sees monopolizer as a "smarty pants" (countertransference)*

    c. *leader angry with group for " abandoning me " by leaving 5 minutes early (countertransference)*

5 minutes 4. Problems we want help with:

    a. *recognizing transferences and countertransferences when they occur*

    b. *help in using facilitating questions*

    c. *drawing out the silent member*

    d. *adjusting to a new member*

Evaluation of Supervisors' assistance:

1. Helped us to organize our presentation and told us when to move on to the next part of our presentation.

2. Pointed out our progress in recognizing transferences and countertransferences; suggested we go through our recordings to see what group events seem to evoke our under- or overreactions.

3. Explored reasons for silence of member; agreed new member was probably uncomfortable and would talk when ready.

4. Suggested facilitative questions, e.g., "What are your thoughts?" rather than, "Do you agree?"

5. Asked questions when they needed more information; put us at ease by not confronting us or being negative.

6. Helped us to see how we were competing for the group's approval.

Figure 6
Group Peer Supervisor Form

Supervisors: *S.C., J.B.*   Supervisees: *C.G., S.T.*

Date of Supervision: *12/11/77*   Type of Group: *Sensory Motor*

Supervision of *3rd group session*   *Stimulation for 5-year-olds*

1. Problems supervisees encountered with this session

    monopolizing
    vying for leader's attention
    limited attention span
    high leader anxiety

2. Themes supervisees identified

    competition, fantasy

3. Themes identified through supervision

    competition between coleaders
    denial of group feeling

4. Transferences and countertransferences

    leader acted protectively toward Tommy
       (countertransference)
    Tommy looked to leader as parent (transference)
    leader angry with monopolizer
       ("smarty pants")
    leader angry with group for leaving early

5. Problems supervisees want assistance with

   recognizing transferences and
       countertransferences;
   using facilitating questions;
   drawing out silent member;
   new member

6. Suggestions we made to supervisees:

   go through process recordings for evidences
       of transferences and countertransferences
   not to use questions that can be answered
       with a "yes" or "no"
   that silent member may be anxious

7. Evaluation of supervisees' presentation:

   Needed minimal direction in presenting data;
       presented clear, relevant information
       in all four areas.
   Showed ability to question their behavior
       and listen to our ideas without using
       denial.
   showed ability to apply group concepts and
       to identify group process.
   We think they did an excellent job!

supervisee is competitive, reluctant, anxious, dependent, or angry, it is most likely that the same struggles are occurring within the group led by that supervisee.

Because group leaders may feel quite unsure about their effectiveness as leaders, they may be hesitant to participate in the supervisory process. Presenting one's work to others is bound to create some anxiety in the group leader. Also, the inexperienced group leader may be alarmed to find that she has some of the same feelings about being in the group that other group members have. For example, the leader of a new group may feel just as anxious in the beginning as the group members do; or the leader may feel anger, sadness, or guilt that parallels group members' feelings when a group experience ends. The student group leader often devalues her contributions to a group experience and may feel quite guilty and frustrated about her leadership accomplishments or her sense of relief that the experience is over. Anger, too, can be experienced by the group leader who feels that termination of the group also terminates a chance to learn and to experience satisfaction; these feelings of loss may be expressed as anger toward the group supervisor, school, or agency, who are viewed as depriving the student leader of a good learning experience. Because some of these feelings may be strong and uncomfortable, the novice group leader may try to act as if she does not have them. She often has a tendency to censor data or to try to escape from exposing her thoughts. It is important for group leaders to talk through their difficulties with a supervisor to lessen the potential for acting out their feelings in the group.

Graduate nurses often lead groups as part of their professional role. If the nurse desires to develop further her group leadership skills, she needs to obtain adequate clinical supervision, which should be supplied by the employing agency. If no expert group leader is available at the agency, the less experienced nurse leader can ask that the agency purchase supervision from a nursing group consultant or be paid for as part of a continuing education program. Or, the agency should provide funds and time for the nurse to obtain supervision on a private basis. Ongoing supervision is especially important when the nurse leads a supportive or therapeutic group; a brief course in group dynamics cannot provide the nurse with all the skills necessary to be a proficient leader.

Regardless of the level of skill or experience of a group leader, certain processes and leader signals point to the need for supervision. If the leader answers in the affirmative to any of the following questions, she probably needs supervision:

Do problems arise in beginning a new group?
Are tension or anxiety levels in the group high?
Is conflict that is not useful proliferating?
Is the group apathetic?
Is decision making unilateral or fragmented?
Is leadership autocratic?
Is the group lacking in cohesiveness?
Does the group continue in the orientation phase for more than six sessions?
Do one or more members always monopolize group sessions?
Is one group member being scapegoated?
Are silences always broken by the leader?
Are new members about to enter the group?
Do group members leave the group abruptly?
Are members absent frequently?
Does physically aggressive behavior occur in the group?
Are group members primarily nonverbal?
Is the group approaching termination?
Does the group seem unable to reach its goals no matter what is tried?

Apart from group-process signals that point to a need for supervision, group-leader signals may also indicate a need for assistance from an experienced group leader. Many factors in the leader's social, educational, or work life can make her more susceptible to group pressures and precipitate countertransference reactions in both the novice and in the experienced leader. One is the presence of reality events in the leader's life situation that may be placing added stress on her. Another is the leader's need to be successful or to be recognized as competent; when the group members show anger or frustration rather than expressing praise or appreciation, the leader may have countertransference reactions. Still another factor is a past significant relationship between the leader and the group, which can force her to play a role yet may impair her ability to see this role as the group sees it. Finally, countertransference reactions in the leader can result from the communication of individual or group anxiety to the leader; to prevent this, the leader needs to know how to differentiate her own anxiety about the group from the anxiety transmitted by the group. Unless the novice group leader learns to deal with the countertransference response adequately, she may leave a group prematurely, or feel guilty, disappointed, or frightened. For this reason, the beginning leader needs to take responsibility for seeking out adequate supervision. One way to do this is to share her perceptions and reactions in classroom discussion with an advisor rather than discussing the exact sentence-by-sentence exchange that occurred in the group. Another way is to ask for individual appointment time with a more experienced group leader or to submit written or taped recordings and ask for assistance in analyzing the situation that brought the countertransference about.

The beginning group leader may feel angry when her unrealistic goals for group movement are not met. Some leaders report overwhelming feelings of guilt, followed by irritation and eventual apathy when group members do not respond as the leaders had hoped they would. Sometimes the irritation and anger are forced underground, and the leader may end up being overprotective of group members or unable to stick firmly to limits for group behavior. One of the most frequent signs of countertransference is a feeling of physical illness or discomfort: diarrhea, muscular aches, headaches, or even persistent colds. Other important symptoms are an inability to focus on what is happening in the group, which can lead to a rejecting attitude toward group members, or other strong positive or negative feelings. Whatever the signs and symptoms, the group leader, especially the novice, who becomes aware that countertransference is occurring needs to seek out supervision.

COLEADERSHIP

The question of whether there should be one or two (or even multiple) leaders of a group is a moot point. Some leaders prefer to work with another person; others feel that working alone is best for them. Agency requirements may dictate coleadership. In some teaching institutions, it is common practice to pair a more experienced group leader with a novice. This arrangement provides the less experienced leader with a role model to imitate. In other institutions, two trainees are paired, in the hope that they will learn from each other.

Coleading a group with another person has advantages and disadvantages that need to be considered carefully prior to starting work with the group, because this type of leadership creates a more complex situation than individual leadership. In general, it is not recommended that leaders work in teams casually; the two leaders must be as seriously committed to working on the relationship between themselves as to working on that between themselves and the group members. In addition, the supervisory process must be relentlessly focused on the coleader relationship, since teams are particularly vulnerable to transference and countertransference reactions. Having two leaders gives the group an opportunity to try to play one leader off against the other, in much the same way as a child turns to his father when his mother denies his request.

Another difficulty of coleading a group is that the leader who talks the most, the one who has the most group experience, or the one toward whom the group has the most positive transference feelings may end up being perceived as the senior leader, and the other will be seen as the junior person. This situation can create tension, because the group will be uncertain about the leaders' roles. The difficulty can sometimes be dealt with to some extent by having the coleaders interview prospective group members together.

Coleading can have disadvantages when efficient use of leaders is an important factor. The group size cannot be doubled just because another leader is added. Therefore, only half the number of groups can be run as when there is only one leader per group. Coleading is also not useful in a group with very young children, because they are often unable to relate to more than one adult at a time.

Lastly, any disagreement or strain between leaders is quickly sensed by the group. This situation is analogous to another family phenomenon wherein the children of fighting parents may react by trying to mediate, by feeling guilty because they think they may be the cause of the disagreement, by withdrawing as if trying to escape the situation, or by "acting up" to direct the parents' anger toward them instead of toward each other. Any of these group reactions can be counterproductive because members use their energy in trying to help the leaders instead of working at their task. Anxiety and inhibited group functioning may be an offshoot of leader disagreement. Trying to hide a disagreement will not be helpful either, because undercover disagreement can be as destructive as open disagreement, if not more so. At the same time, coleaders need to acknowledge the probability of some disagreement, since this occurs whenever two individuals attempt to form a relationship.

Although these disadvantages of coleadership are very real, ways can be found to decrease the potential for group movement to be hampered by them. In the first place, the coleaders should meet before the sessions begin for the sole purpose of becoming acquainted with each other as people. Openness and respect should prevail. Each leader could draw up a list of questions he wishes to ask the other. There is bound to be some difference in their approaches to group interventions, but the differences should not be so great that the two cannot work together. The coleaders might discuss such questions as:

What are your goals for this group?
What is your theoretical orientation to group leading?
How do you see yourself functioning in this group?

How do you see me functioning in this group?

What group-leader strengths do you think you have?

What group-leader weaknesses do you think you have?

What suggestions do you have for handling possible disagreements between us in the group?

Do you think we will try to compete with each other and, if so, how can we recognize and deal with this to keep it from interfering with group movement?

How do you feel about our seeking out supervision?

How could we present group data to a supervisor?

What are your thoughts about how we can deal with such group problems as monopolizing, scapegoating, silence, new members, transferences, physical aggression, nonverbal members, absences, and manipulation?

One or more meetings prior to the beginning of the coleadership experience can decrease the likelihood that each coleader will try to meet her own needs rather than the needs of the group. If the coleaders wish to continue to monitor their activities in the group, they could meet together after each session to review group process, validate one another's perceptions of group events, identify special needs of the group, and identify areas of growth and the need for supervision of the coleaders. Ideally, at least, some of these postmeeting sessions should include a more experienced group leader.

One purpose of the postmeeting session is to give the leaders a chance to deal with any disagreement they may have about how to handle the group process. During the orientation phase it is not wise to attempt to try to settle any disagreement within the group context, since the focus at this stage of group development is on the establishment of a sense of trust in the leaders. Many coleaders continue to deal with any disagreements outside of the group even later in the group process. This approach is reminiscent of that taken by parents who discuss problems in their relationship when children are not present. On the other hand, some coleaders have begun to think that if their disagreements can take place within the group, in an atmosphere of trust and respect, they can teach group members how to disagree yet continue to work together effectively. If the leaders can manage this, the groups could have powerful learning experiences in effective interpersonal relationships. However, this approach should be used with caution. It should not be attempted unless the coleaders have worked through their relationship so as to be able to disagree without becoming angry; in most cases this requires supervision and practice.

Coleading does offer several advantages over single leadership. (1) Novice group leaders can observe a more experienced leader in action, and they can gradually assume leadership functions as they become comfortable in those roles. Moving from a more structured, dependent role to a less structured, interdependent role can provide support and decrease the anxiety level of the beginning leader. (2) The inexperienced leader who works with a more experienced group observer has an opportunity to validate her perceptions of group process. (3) Coleaders can act as role models for the group by demonstrating how to communicate clearly, cooperate, collaborate, and disagree effectively. (4) The coleadership relationship re-creates the family situation of mother and father; such a re-creation can be especially useful when working with parents, families, or children. Regardless of the leaders' sex, they can be perceived as parental figures by group members, thus making transference reactions clearer and more easily identifiable. (5) Coleaders can act in complementary roles, each reenforcing the other. For example, one can act as nonverbal observer of group process for one session, while the other is verbal and directs group interaction. The nurse who acts as nonverbal observer may also serve as recorder for that session. In postmeeting sessions, the observer/recorder can give her coleader helpful feedback on group process. For the next session, the two may reverse these roles, or not. In the latter case, there is less need to work out the relationship within the group, but time is required to work out how continuity will be maintained when leaders do alternate roles. Even though the pair may seem to be working as a single leader, there is still a tendency to compete with one another as leaders, to compare one's leading style with one's partners, and to disagree about how to approach group problems. It is not unusual for group members to try to create a division between the group leaders by complimenting that day's leader, by complaining about last week's leader, or by acting in ways divisive to the leadership pair. For these reasons, postmeeting sessions can be helpful even in a complementary role arrangement.

Another way a pair of leaders can work together in a group is for one leader to focus on the group process, while the other focuses on individual members. This approach can be especially effective with individual group members who may need more structured situations. In such cases, one leader can move around the group, orienting confused group members to group events, providing physical and emotional support by sitting next to anxious or disruptive group members, and by setting limits on disruptive behavior. A final advantage of the coleadership situation is that it allows the group to continue during the absence of one of the leaders.

SIMULATED EXERCISES

Each of the two simulated exercises that follow includes an experiential and a discussion section. If either exercise is completed without an instructor or supervisor present, participants should plan to share difficulties and insights with a more experienced group leader following the completion of the exercises.

Exercise 1

Assertive Behavior

This skill exercise can be used whenever participants find it difficult to state their wishes, desires, or needs in an assertive way. Peer supervision is a component of this exercise.

The exercise helps to develop skill in "I" assertive presentations of self. Withdrawal and/or "You" aggressive responses are replaced by clear, consistent messages.

Each person is to identify one situation where she wishes she had been able to say, "This is what I think," "This is what I feel," or "This is what I want."

Objectives

1. To identify interpersonal situations in which aggressive or withdrawal behavior was used.

2. To practice giving "I" assertive messages.

3. To practice giving feedback to others about their communication.

Procedure

1. The group or the instructor appoints a timekeeper, who makes sure that agreed-upon time limits for each step are observed. The timekeeper is also responsible for warning the group when five minutes are left to accomplish the task.

10-15 minutes

2. The larger group breaks into pairs. One person in the pair briefs the other on the situation from which she withdrew or became aggressive instead of assertive. The first person then practices saying, in an assertive manner, whatever it was she was not able to say that way in the actual situation. The second gives her feedback to help bring out assertiveness: "Look me in the eye when you say that," or "Don't laugh when you say that," or "Your words say one thing but your face says another."

10-15 minutes

3. The leader asks the pairs to reverse roles and the second person in the pair briefs the other person on the situation in which she was unable to be assertive. The pairs then proceed as described in number 2 above.

4. The entire group reconvenes and discusses the simulations, focusing on the following points:

15-30
minutes

a. How did it feel to be assertive?

b. What prevented each person from being assertive in the original situation? Were their fears realistic?

c. What was learned from this exercise that can be applied in other situations?

Exercise 2

Peer Supervision

This exercise is useful for developing skills as peer supervisor and peer supervisee.

Objectives

1. To learn to use supervisory time efficiently by focusing on the issues of themes, transferences, countertransferences, problems encountered in the group, and problems that cannot be solved without assistance.
2. To practice presenting group-process data verbally.
3. To practice commenting on others' data presentations in a nonthreatening way.

Procedure

1. The larger group breaks into subgroups of five; two will have the role of supervisor, two will be supervisees, and one will be timekeeper.

2. Each subgroup appoints one of its members to be the timekeeper, who is responsible for making sure that the supervisees present data for no more than 20 minutes.

3. The supervisees (or coleaders) are directed by the timekeeper to begin presenting data to the group, but first to look at the guide on page 106 of this book. Meanwhile, the timekeeper briefs the other two group members on their roles as supervisors.

5-30 minutes

4. The timekeeper tells the supervisors to follow the guide on page 106 when taking notes on the supervisee(s) presentation. The supervisors are to ensure that all four areas are covered during the 20-minute presentation period. If supervisees spend too much or too little time on any area, the supervisors (coached by the timekeeper) are to redirect the presentation with comments such as: "Let's move on to countertransferences now," "What about themes?" or "Tell us some more about the problems in the group that we might be able to help you with."

20 minutes

5. When both supervisee(s) and supervisors are ready to begin, the timekeeper begins timing the presentation, warns the group when only five minutes of presentation time remain, and calls time when 20 minutes have elapsed.

20 minutes

6. Supervisors criticize the supervisee(s)' presentation, give suggestions for handling group problems, point out omissions in data, and compliment the presenter(s) on strengths.

10-30
minutes

7. Each member of the group is asked by the timekeeper to tell what was learned from this experience and in what ways peer supervisors or supervisees could have been more effective in their roles.

PEER GROUP SUPERVISION PRESENTATION GUIDE

You have 20 minutes to present data about one or more group sessions you have led. Be sure to cover all four areas below in the alloted time period.

Group themes

Group problems (monopolizing, scapegoating, anxiety, conflict, decision making, and so on)

Transferences and countertransferences

Problems the leader(s) need help with

READINGS

Allen, James. "Peer Group Supervision in Family Therapy," *Child Welfare* 55(1975): 423-439.

Armony, Nahmna. "Countertransference: Obstacle and Instrument," *Contemporary Psychoanalysis* 11(1975): 265-281.

Burnside, Irene. "Peer Supervision: A Method of Teaching," *Journal of Nursing Education* 10(1971): 15-22.

Clark, Carolyn. "A Social Systems Approach to Short-Term Psychiatric Care," *Perspectives in Psychiatric Care* 10(1972): 178-182.

Fensterheim, Herbert, and Jean Baer. *Don't Say Yes When You Want to Say No.* New York: Dell, 1975.

Fuchs, Lester. "Reflections on Touching and Transference in Psychotherapy," *Clinical Social Work Journal* 3(1975): 167-176.

Morrow, Robert. "Symposium: Ethnic Differences in Therapeutic Relationships," *Professional Psychology* 6(1975): 468-469.

Kabcenell, Robert. "On Countertransference," *Psychoanalytic Study of the Child* 29(1974): 27-33.

Lane, Ross. "The Influence of Supervision on Trainee's Development of Facilitative Skills in Counseling," *Dissertation Abstracts International* 34(1974): 4748-4749.

Semmelroth, Carl, and Sara Semmelroth. "The Need for Better Supervision among Mental Health Professionals," *Improving Human Performance Quarterly* 4(1975): 37-42.

Smith, Manuel. *When I Say No, I Feel Guilty.* New York: Dial, 1975.

Taubman, Bryna. *How To Become an Assertive Woman.* New York: Pocket Books, 1976.

Termini, Marguerite, and Marilyn Hauser. "The Process of the Supervisory Relationship," *Perspectives in Psychiatric Care* 11(1973): 121-125.

6

Behavioral Approaches for Group Leaders

The term "behavioral modification" or "the behavioral approach" refers to an approach that focuses on behavioral change and is based on certain principles of learning, such as reinforcement. To some extent, all communication can be said to be behaviorally oriented, since it usually represents an attempt to influence others. The leader who nods in approval when a group member speaks reinforces that behavior, thus increasing the possibility that it will occur more frequently. The behavioral approach is not concerned with insight or with whether the person understands why he acts as he does, but it focuses on decreasing unsatisfying or disruptive behavior and on increasing satisfying, goal-directed behavior.

A behavioral approach considers the individual's present difficulties, identifies specific behaviors that must be changed, counts the frequency of each behavior (baseline data), and then uses reinforcement to increase desired behaviors. The behavioral approach can be used in a number of ways in a group setting. One way is to gather together a group of either staff members or clients in order to teach them assertive behavior. Behavioral modification techniques can also be used to help one or more group members to make more verbal statements, or to decrease disruptive behavior in others. Yet another way to use this approach is to gather together parents who are concerned about their children's behavior. Common behavioral patterns that can be dealt with by teaching parents certain behavioral approaches include complaining, soiling, teasing, truancy, temper tantrums, sulking, not picking up toys or possessions, and crying.

ASSERTIVENESS

An assertive person demonstrates through words and actions that "This is what I think. This is what I feel. This is what I want." Assertive people set goals, act on achieved goals in a clear and consistent way, and take responsibility for the consequences of those actions. In contrast, aggressive behavior has a controlling or manipulating aspect that is often hidden, out of proportion to the relationships, or off the point of discussion. In assertive behavior, a person states and stands up for his rights, knowing full well that others may disagree or attempt to block his action. The assertive person gives clear and open messages about what is desired.

Giving "I" Messages

The first way a leader can help a group to become less aggressive or withdrawn and more assertive is to teach the members to give "I" messages. Such messages convey how the individual thinks or feels: "I can't help you now." "I don't like to be shouted at." "I believe your figures are wrong." "I want to talk this over with you." "I feel angry." "I feel guilty about being late." "I feel uncomfortable." "(I) thank you." "I disagree with that." These "I"-assertive messages are definitely different from "you"-aggressive messages that place blame on the other person, who then tends to become defensive: "You know I'm busy." "Don't you shout at me!" "Can't you ever add this up right?"

"You don't know what you're talking about!" "Stop meddling in my work." "Why do you always start the group so early?" "Why are you always picking on me?" When increasing assertiveness is a goal, the leader should stop any member who gives a "You" message during a session and ask him to restate it in "I"-message form.

CHANGING UNWANTED HABITS

An experienced group leader can teach group members how to identify and change unwanted habits. Five steps are involved in developing this skill.

The first step is to express the habit in behaviors that can be counted or measured. For example, if the objective is to increase one's ability to communicate effectively with coworkers, one could count frequency of direct eye contact, loudness and firmness of the speaking voice, and whether the speaker sticks to the point or makes qualifying statements—"I'm sorry, but . . ." or "This is probably not right, but . . . ."

The next step is to count the selected behaviors over at least a week's time. This data will give the person a baseline to use in checking progress in changing the habit.

The third step is to determine what precedes the unwanted habit behavior. For example, does the person have difficulty only when speaking with coworkers in a group setting, or only when speaking to a certain coworker? Is there a beginning or midpoint at which the habitual behavior could be interrupted? At what point does it seem impossible to interrupt the habitual behavior?

The fourth step is to have the individual make a contract of intention to change the habit. In this case, group members can make contracts with other group members. Contracts may be verbal or written, but they should contain simple, attainable goals. A reasonable beginning contract might be: "I will look directly into the group leader's eyes when speaking to her." Once the objective of this contract has been met for several sessions, it can be expanded to include looking into all group members' eyes when speaking to them. Each time a contract is fulfilled, the next contract can be aimed at correcting more difficult behaviors. When all the group members' counted behaviors have been changed, the leader can set up role-playing situations in which a group member describes a coworker with whom she has been unable to communicate directly. Practice sessions using tape recordings and/or videotape can give the group member feedback about how well she communicates with others. The group member can then practice communicating directly with the person playing the coworker role. Finally, the contract can be extended to include extragroup behaviors with the real coworker.

The final step in the process is to try to arrange the environmental elements so that the goal will be easy to reach. For example, approaching coworkers for discussions might be most fruitful when all concerned are neither rushed nor fatigued.

INCREASING COOPERATIVE BEHAVIORS

Group members who are unusually noisy, inattentive, or nonverbal are prime candidates for taking on the scapegoat role. As soon as the leader notices that a group member does not sit still, leaves the group, loudly interrupts others, or does not speak clearly, this should be a signal to begin to plan an intervention, perhaps using the behavioral approach.

In this approach, the leader's first task is to differentiate between behaviors that are deviative and those that are cooperative. For example, some deviating behaviors in a group might be getting out of one's chair, interrupting while another person is talking, and not answering when asked a question.

The second task is to record baseline data. This kind of data gives the answers to several questions. How often during a certain time unit does the group member get out of his chair? How often per time unit does he interrupt another person? How often per time unit does he fail to answer when asked a question?

Several group sessions will probably be needed to establish the average frequency of each behavior. This baseline data need not be kept a secret. In fact, people are sometimes influenced to change their behavior just by knowing how frequently a certain action occurs. The noncooperative member or other group members can be enlisted in this data-collecting procedure, depending on the leader's judgment.

The next step is to pinpoint the events that precede the unwanted behaviors being studied. Often the leader or other group members may be instrumental in setting off noncooperative behavior. For example, the leader may reinforce a group member's disruptive comment by paying undue attention to it; this is often a signal for the member to continue being disruptive. It may be assumed that there are some current rewarding consequences of the behavior. The leader might formulate several functional hypotheses regarding what particular reinforcement is maintaining the noncooperative behavior and then test these out through observation and experimentation. Although she may have hunches about what the member finds rewarding in his noncooperative behavior, it is imperative that such rewards should not be removed during the baseline data-gathering period.

Many reinforcers—a smile, a nod, or a grimace—would seem to have low influence, yet they can maintain a group member's behavior. The leader's task as interventionist is to alter the milieu so that the most powerful reinforcers will be those that strengthen cooperative behavior.

One way to find out what is reinforcing or rewarding to a group member may be to ask him; during or after a group session, the leader might ask some or all of the following questions: "What do you like to do best?" "What would make it more pleasant for you in the group?" "Which person in the group do you feel most comfortable with?" If the group member can answer any or all of these questions, the leader can then begin to formulate ideas about how to elicit cooperative behavior from him. For example, if he says that getting up from his chair relieves tension, the leader might contract with him that he can get up for one minute after each question he answers with three or more words. This contract may be verbal or written. In carrying out the contract, the leader may involve the group in giving support to cooperative behavior. She might say something like, "We have a group problem to help Tom learn how to answer questions more effectively. I've devised a plan that may work. Wendy, will you keep track of the number of words, make sure he gets to take his prize of being out of his chair for one minute." When it is difficult to engage the group in assisting with the contract, the leader could try the token system, in which members who volunteer to assist with the contract may earn tokens or other privileges. The leader decides whether or not the tokens can be turned in later for more concrete rewards, such as candy, cake, a group termination party, or some other reward decided on by the group.

When working with a group of children or adolescents, the leader can ask parents to provide reinforcers. Allowances, television viewing, or other special privileges can be granted by the parents when they receive a note or call from the leader indicating that a reward has been earned. When working with others in providing rewards, the leader needs to structure the relationship so that whoever else is involved also gets rewarded for being consistent in dispensing rewards. If this facet is not considered, parents or others will not be motivated to collaborate.

Whether a contract is written or verbal, it may be to the leader's advantage to enlist the support of other group members in helping the noncooperative member count the words in his answer and making sure he takes his reward of getting out of his chair. Thus other group members are cast in the role of helping, supportive, and cooperative persons, and they are less likely to scapegoat the noncooperative member because they will be rewarded by the group leader's comments and praise for their efforts.

Another way to involve all group members in the contract is to use charts or graphs to show progress toward the goal. Stars, checks, or other measures of progress can be used by the leader or by other group members to demonstrate and reinforce concrete movement toward a goal. The leader may wish to comment to the group on a member's progress as a further reward for movement toward more appropriate behavior.

Involving the group as reinforcers will only work when several factors have been considered. First, the group must be able to dispense the reinforcers. If the noncooperative member says that the only thing that pleases him is a hot fudge sundae, and he is on a diabetic diet, the reinforcer cannot be dispensed. Then, the group may have to search for other reinforcers by observing what pleases him, or even by asking family members or friends what pleases him. Second, the reinforcer can only be given as stated in the contract. Also, the reward must be given each time the cooperative behavior occurs, without exception, since it is the consistency of the reinforcing response that will maintain the cooperative behavior. Additional reinforcers may also develop in time; for example, other group members will probably become more friendly toward him, and this new reinforcer will help to maintain the cooperative behavior. A third factor that needs to be considered is the way the leader presents the contract. She must be careful to present it in a matter-of-fact, nonpunitive style, with no verbal or nonverbal comments about noncooperative behavior, since the purpose of the contract is to reward cooperative behavior. The leader concentrates on changing one behavior before moving on to the next target behavior. For this reason, the most disturbing behavior is dealt with first. In the example given above, the getting-out-of-seat behavior may decrease simply due to satiation; that is, the group member may be able to get out of his seat—and in fact is encouraged to do so—whenever he wishes to answer with three words or more. At a certain point, getting out of his chair may become more of a task than a reward. Once other group members start reinforcing his verbalizations, he may learn that talking can be more pleasurable than leaving the group circle.

In addition to using reinforcers to promote wanted behaviors, the group leader can use behavioral modification techniques to help members develop new behaviors. One such technique is called shaping. Shaping is the reinforcement of successive approximations toward the desired behavior. For example, if the goal is to get one member to talk to another group member, the first desirable behavior may be to look at that person.

By praising or rewarding the member for first looking at another group member, the leader can shape behavior in the desired direction. Other desirable behaviors, such as maintaining eye contact and saying hello to the other, would also be praised. The idea of shaping is that each small step toward the goal is praised, and thus the group member slowly develops the entire repertoire needed to achieve the goal in the end.

A second behavioral modification technique is prompting. The leader tells the group member how to perform one or more steps in the desired behavior pattern. For example: "Look at Sally now; look right in her eyes and say hello." The techniques of prompting and shaping are frequently combined to achieve an appropriate response.

Modeling is another useful behavioral modification technique. In modeling, the leader demonstrates the desired behaviors. For example, the leader might say, "Watch me as I talk with Karen." Modeling can also be used more indirectly. Group members naturally imitate significant other people; thus, as a significant person in the group, the leader models behavior whenever she teaches the group how to interact by interacting with them. The leader might also use as role models group members who are proficient in a skill.

Another behavioral modification technique is the use of incompatible responses. This can be used when the desired behavior is incompatible with the undesired behavior. For example, the undesired behavior in a teaching group may be classroom disruption. Therefore, the target behavior may be academic performance. The rationale for choosing to focus on academic performance is that adequate performance in this area is incompatible with classroom disruption. The initial behavior required to be eligible for a reward should be easily attainable. A beginning behavior might be to open a book or to hold learning materials. Once the disruptive member has attained this goal, a more complex goal, such as reading two paragraphs of the book or learning the purpose of one piece of equipment, will be sufficient to receive the reward. Gradually, the level of accomplishment is raised to include understanding of more complex learning material.

WORKING WITH PARENTS

Until recently, parenting was thought of as an innate skill. Now it seems an accepted fact that people do need assistance in learning to be effective parents. The group setting can be an especially productive environment for learning parenting skills, since parents can learn from one another as well as from the leader.

Some skills parents can learn in group sessions are how to praise and give reinforcers for appropriate behavior, how to ignore deviant or inappropriate behavior, and how to implement three-minute "time-out" periods. The time-out period may consist of having the child go to his room to be alone for the time specified, or removing him from a pleasurable situation such as watching television or playing with his toys.

A group of parents can be taught how to specify behaviors, collect baseline data, select reinforcers, and develop contracts. While group members are collecting data at home, one or more of the problem behaviors can be selected by the leader for the group to explore. Parents whose children do not have that specific behavioral problem can model what they would do to handle the problem. The rest of the group can give feedback to the modeling parents, ask questions, and discuss their own difficulties in handling that problem.

Subsequent group sessions might be used to discuss difficulties and successes in using various behavioral approaches in the actual parenting situation. The leader will probably also have to deal with family resistance to certain behavioral modification methods. Such resistance is most likely to occur when parental discord and family disorganization is ongoing and chronic. In these instances, parents habitually provide inconsistent and contradictory cues to their children. When the leader notes that this is the case, she refers the family for marital-pair psychotherapy, a type of therapy that deals with basic parental conflict. Another source of resistance occurs when parents insist that all children should be treated alike, without favoritism. Although parents frequently claim to practice nonfavoritism, they often individualize punishment. In such cases, the leader can try to extend behavioral modification techniques to include all the children. Another family resistance is related to the "needed family scapegoat" phenomenon. Here, the child's problem behavior serves a highly complex purpose in the family; as a result, when the behavior of this sibling improves, forms of disturbance or friction may appear in other family members. In such instances, parents should be referred to a family therapist. A nearly universal resistance to behavioral modification is the philosophy of not wanting to control another person's life. Parents frequently wish to be friends with their children, or at least hope to be viewed as permissive, progressive parents, and the group leader may need to present oral or written material about how parents reward and punish behavior in any case. What the behavioral approach teaches is how to reward positive behavior consistently and effectively.

SIMULATED EXERCISES

Two simulated exercises follow. Both are skill exercises, and for each a list of discussion questions is given. If the group is larger that 15, it should be divided into equal-size subgroups. When an experienced group leader is not present during the discussion session, a postexercise session should be held with a supervisor or instructor to discuss difficulties encountered.

Exercise 1

Preparing for Changes

This skill exercise can be used whenever a change such as termination, entrance of a new group member, or movement from one group phase to another is anticipated. It can also be used to increase flexibility to unknown change situations, since a problem-solving approach is taught.

The purpose of the exercise is to gain skill in planning for change, whether it is an anticipated or an unanticipated change. Changes are examined using a problem-solving approach that can be transferred to real-life situations.

Objectives

1. To learn a problem-solving approach to change.

2. To practice preparing for upcoming changes.

Procedure

1. The group appoints a timekeeper, who makes sure that time limits for each step are observed. Together, the group decides on what time limits will be used. The timekeeper orients the group at each step regarding how much time remains for the task.

2. The group or the instructor appoints a leader for each group.

10 minutes

3. The leader asks each group member to write down on a piece of paper a real or hypothetical change, one thing she would like to learn from the change, one thing she would like to produce as a result of the change, and one reward or satisfaction she would like to experience as a result of the change.

30-60 minutes

4. The leader asks each group member in turn to tell the other group members what the change is, what is to be learned or produced, and what reward would be helpful. The leader then asks the group member what barriers there are to reaching the goal, what alternatives the person has, what resources she has, and what further planning for change is needed. If the group member is unable to answer any or all of these questions, the leader can ask, "Who in the group has a suggestion for this?"

15-45 minutes

5. The leader assists the group to discuss the following points:
   a. What is difficult about change?
   b. What could be rewarding about change?
   c. Is change seen by the majority of group members as satisfying? If no, why not? If yes, what opinions does the group have about this?

d. What barriers seem to be mentioned most by group members? What ideas does the group have about why these barriers are mentioned most often? What can be done to remove barriers to change?
e. What seems to prevent group members from stating alternative actions or from identifying untapped resources?
f. What was learned from this exercise that can be applied in other situations?

Exercise 2

Teaching

This exercise can be used whenever the nurse leader requires skill in teaching others. The purpose of the exercise is to help the leader gain skill in preparing and delivering information to others. Skill in giving feedback to others' teaching efforts is also enhanced.

This exercise requires a great deal of preparation. Prior to undertaking it, each group member must be familiar with the content of the material to be taught and must have thought about how she wishes to present a five-minute segment of the material to the group. Source materials, as well as the additional readings section at the end of this chapter, may be consulted.

Objectives

1. To identify a topic suitable to be taught in the group format.

2. To list factors that need to be considered when teaching others.

3. To practice teaching in a group format.

4. To give and receive feedback on teaching skills.

Procedure

1. The group or instructor appoints a leader for each group.

75
minutes
maximum

2. The leader asks each group member in turn to "teach" the rest of the group. The leader does not intervene in each person's teaching but allows it to go on for five minutes and then asks the group for helpful hints on teaching the content chosen. The leader also asks the group for feedback to the group member who taught on the following: What are important things to consider in teaching a group this material? What types of resources need to be considered? Does the teacher need to do further research on the content of her presentation? What principles of learning need to be considered further? What problems seem to be inherent in this teaching situation?

20-60
minutes

3. When every group member has finished her presentation and received feedback, the leader assists the group to discuss the following questions:
   a. How does readiness affect learning?
   b. How can the teacher find out what the learner already knows?
   c. How does the teacher assess whether the presentation is too technical, complex, fast, or slow for the learner?
   d. How can anxiety affect learning? What can the leader or teacher do to decrease anxiety in the group?

121

e. How can repetition and feedback be built into a teaching program?
f. What kind of media and equipment could be used to teach the material most effectively?
g. How can the teacher assist group members to share information with one another and participate in the teaching-learning experience?
h. What was learned from this exercise that can be applied in other situations?

READINGS

Berni, Rosemarian, and Wilbert Fordyce. *Behavior Modification and the Nursing Process.* St. Louis, Mo.: C.V. Mosby, 1973.

Clark, Carolyn. "Learning Through Teaching," *Nursing Concepts and Processes.* Albany, N.Y.: Delmar Publishers, 1977.

Fensterheim, Herbert, and Jean Baer. *Don't Say Yes When You Want To Say No.* New York: Dell, 1975.

Gordon, Thomas. *Parent Effectiveness Training.* New York: New American Library, 1970.

Krumboltz, John, and Helen Krumboltz. *Changing Children's Behavior.* Englewood Cliffs, N.J.: Prentice-Hall, 1972.

Laird, Mona. "Techniques for Teaching Pre- and Postoperative Patients," *American Journal of Nursing* 75(1975): 1338-1340.

LeBow, Michael. *Approaches to Modifying Patient Behavior.* New York: Appleton-Century-Crofts, 1976.

Loomis, Maxine, and JoAnne Horsley. *Interpersonal Change: A Behavioral Approach to Nursing Practice.* New York: McGraw-Hill, 1974.

Mash, Eric, Lee Handy, and Leo Hanerlynck, eds. *Behavior Modification Approaches to Parenting.* New York: Brunner/Mazel, 1976.

Pratt, Sandra, and Joel Fischer. "Behavior Modification: Changing Hyperactive Behavior in a Children's Group," *Perspectives in Psychiatric Care* 12(1975): 37-42.

Salzer, Joan. "Classes to Improve Diabetic Self-Care," *American Journal of Nursing* 75(1975): 1324-1326.

Smyth, Kathleen, ed. "Symposium on Patient Teaching," *Nursing Clinics of North America* 6(1970): 571-806.

Tharp, Roland, and Ralph Wetzel. *Behavior Modification in the Natural Environment.* New York: Academic Press, 1969.

7

Recording

RECORDING IS IMPORTANT

Recording group interactions for study is important for a number of reasons. First, recording the multitude of verbal and non-verbal communications as they occur in a group meeting decreases the chances of omitting important details, since recall of events decreases rapidly with time. Second, recording what happens in the group will allow the group leader to review what happened within and across group sessions. Third, recording group interactions will help the leader to review her group skills, to compare them with those she has previously demonstrated at other sessions, and to evaluate her progress as a group leader. Fourth, recording will encourage the leader to think of what has been said or done in various group interactions, and this will increase her potential for dealing more effectively with similar situations in the future.

RECORDING METHODS

A number of methods can be utilized for recording group interactions for later study. Three of the most useful types of records are (1) the written record, (2) audiotape recordings, and (3) videotape recordings.

Some group participants may become anxious when they learn that a permanent record is being made of their behavior. The group recorder can usually prevent or decrease such anxiety among group members by:

1. Stating in a positive manner that recordings will be made—
    e.g., "I'd like to record what happens in this group so I can learn about how groups work. (Pause.) Any comments?" or, "I'm going to be recording this meeting so I can learn how to be of more help to all of you. Any reactions to this?"
2. Telling the group members with whom the recording will be shared—
    e.g., "I will share the recordings with my instructor and fellow students only," or, "The only people who will hear this tape are my supervisor and your social worker."
3. Playing back a segment of the tape or showing the written notes to participants who seem especially anxious about the recording. This can be done at the end of a meeting or at the time of establishing that recordings will be done, depending on the insistence of the group members. Much anxiety about recordings seems to be related to how participants sound on tape or to the idea that the recorder is recording more than what is actually happening. Once participants hear how they sound on tape and/or what is being recorded, anxiety is minimized.

If none of these techniques works, the group leader is forced either to change the method of recording to one that is more acceptable to the group, or to stop recording. But before doing either of these things, the recorder can inquire, "What is it about recording that you object to?" Sometimes a group member will voice an objection, such as concern about confidentiality, that can be dealt with without stopping the recording. Generally, the group recorder will receive group consensus to record; rarely, if ever, do groups refuse to allow recording if the suggestions given here are followed.

Written Records

To be of most use later, the written record should be made at the time the group meets. Depending on the type of group interaction, the nurse who is recording the information needs to spend some time receiving group consent for this. In committee meetings, where a secretary usually takes notes in any case, there may be little difficulty in receiving group consent. But in supportive groups where members may fear disclosure of their comments it may be more difficult to get their consent to make a written record of the group session.

Once it has been decided that written records will be made, the nurse may need to practice recording before the group sessions actually begin. Experience in this skill can be gained through practice in simulated group situations. To be proficient in recording group interaction, several skills will have to be learned: a coding or symbol system for words or actions that occur frequently, a way to determine what is important to record and what is not, and the ability to observe and write at the same time. Novices at recording often complain of feeling overwhelmed ("There's too much to record"), or they worry that they are unable to tell what is important and what is not important to record ("I can't write down every sigh and frown; how do I know what to record?").

The nurse leader can develop her own coding or symbol system for group interaction. For example, group members can be assigned numbers or initials, anxiety can be represented by a *, or silence by S. Common symbols used in nursing, such as $\bar{c}$ for with, $\bar{s}$ for without, can also be adopted to conserve time and space. Two advantages of the written record method are that little equipment is needed and that tapes need not be replayed after the group meeting in order to evaluate group interaction. Writing in a group may also be less intrusive and more acceptable to group members than would audio- or videotaping. A disadvantage of the written record is that nonverbal messages, such as body posture, eye contact, and gestures, may not be noted if the nurse becomes too involved in recording verbal communication. Usually, the nurse is unable to be a vocal group participant as well, since participating and recording are each a full-time function.

Audiotape Records

Audiotape recording must be done while the group is in session. It is important for the leader to familiarize herself completely with the use of the audiotape equipment before the group meets. Audiovisual, educational technology, or library and learning resources technicians can be approached for assistance in this area. The meeting room should be checked out to make sure it is suitable for recording; in very noisy settings, unwanted sounds may be picked up which can override spoken conversation. The group recorder also has to place the microphone so that it will most effectively pick up all group members' remarks.

Some advantages of audiotaping are that the group recorder is free to join in the group discussion and can then evaluate her leadership skills by listening to the tape at a later date, and that portions can be replayed to teach participants or to refresh memories about what really was said. (Hearing one's own voice make a statement is much less likely to be dismissed than hearing someone read back what was apparently said.) A major disadvantage of the audiotape method is that visual cues, such as gestures or movements, are not available for study. Therefore, the leader may wish to jot down important visual cues for later study. Another disadvantage is that it takes at least twice as long to listen to and evaluate a tape as it does to record the session. However, if the group recorder, instructor, and/or group supervisor is interested in hearing a tape rather than reading a written record, the audiotape may be the method of choice.

Videotape Records

Videotape equipment is used while the group is in session. Becoming proficient in the use of lights, cameras, and other needed equipment is mandatory and may become quite time-consuming. Consequently, the leader may need at first to request the assistance of a videotape technician or an experienced student. Lighting, noise/quietness, space, and other aspects of the environment must be adequately checked out before taping begins.

Some advantages of the videotape are that the group recorder is free to join the session, and a complete record of verbal and nonverbal communication is recorded, exactly as it occurred. Another major advantage of the videotape method is that portions can be played back to the group to demonstrate concepts, to review what was said, or to do on-the-spot teaching of participants. Disadvantages of videotape are that equipment is relatively heavy and unwieldy and not always available, and that, because of the intrusiveness of the method, it may take longer for group members to relax and participate in the group discussion.

THE GROUP RECORDING GUIDE

The Group Recording Guide, which has been tested with more than 100 beginning nurse leaders, was developed as a means of enhancing the leader's observation and leadership skills and recording ability. It tests for all the types of information a group recorder, observer, or leader needs in order to assess group interaction.

Figure 7

Group Recording Guide

Seating Arrangement*:

Date: February 6, 1977

(R): Linda J.

(L): Pat T.

Type and purpose of group:

Reality orientation for nursing home residents

Group Recording Guide

Events	Analysis of Events	Leader Action	Evaluation of Leader Actions	Alternative Actions

*L = leader, R = recorder, ● = empty chairs.

Supplementary Data Needed for
Meaningful Recording

The top half of Figure 7 illustrates the type of supplementary data the leader needs to collect at the beginning of each recording session, before the actual discussion begins. (This part of the form is not repeated on succeeding pages of a single recording.) Seating arrangement may be highly significant, because it can reveal information about that session as well as offer comparison with other sessions. For example, if member number 1 always sits next to the leader, looks to the leader for answers to questions, and never initiates topics for discussion, the leader may well speculate that this member is highly dependent on her. Or if the leader and group recorder always sit next to one another and group members always leave an empty chair between themselves and the "authority figures" (L and R), the nurse may suspect that the group is not one, but is split into factions. Another example of the significance of seating arrangement is seen when an empty chair is always left next to certain members; those group members are probably being isolated by the rest of the group. Or if all couples in a group composed of couples sit together (the norm) with the exception of one, and these two sit one on each side of the leader, what theories might the observer want to test out through observing the session? Seating arrangement may or may not be significant, but the leader, as an observant group member, will want to use all possible group data available to help in improving group function.

Dates of the meetings should be recorded, since there may be need later to trace the sequence of progress from session to session. Also, the names of the group recorder and leader can be used to trace their development of group skills. The type of group and its purpose are recorded to aid readers who are not familiar with the group composition. Figure 8 lists other data to be collected.

Figure 8
The Group Recording Guide

Events	Analysis of Events	Leader Action	Evaluation of Leader Actions	Alternative Actions
all behaviors of group members:	hunches about what the events seemed to mean:	what the leader did, including all behaviors listed in the Events column	all hunches about why leader action was effective or ineffective:	all specific statements of how the leader might more effectively:
words spoken	changes in group atmosphere		introduction sufficient (insufficient)	give responsibility to a group
silences	changes in cohesiveness		group returned to focus of discussion (did not return)	increase security
gestures				keep action moving
tone of voice	distortions of what occurred		tension decreased (increased)	restate
increase or decrease in speech flow	feelings revealed			give information
eye contact	coping devices used		leader's feelings interfered with action	clarify
restless movements	type and/or effect of silences		communication skills used (not used)	point out
facial expressions	dependency			test for consensus
posture	pairing		less talkative people are (are not) talking	summarize
language "hangups"	scapegoating		overtalkative people are quieter (more talkative)	explore
entrance or exit of new member	monopolizing		apathy has decreased (increased)	get information
	characteristic phase behavior			keep to topic
	decisions reached		goals defined (need definition)	
	norms revealed			

group disruption

competition

themes

transferences

leader placed responsibility
with group (did not)

effective (ineffective)
decision making

conflict decreased (increased)

nonuseful (useful) silence

cohesion increased (decreased)

scapegoating ends (continues)

competition ends (continues)

even (uneven) balance between
task and maintenance
functions

Events

Group events are all the behaviors of group members during a
session except those of the formal or designated leader. Since
informal leadership always occurs in groups to some degree,
leadership behavior of informal leaders is placed in the Events
column.

Words that are spoken should be placed in quotation marks,
following the group member's number or initials:

EVENTS

H. G.   "That's a rotten thing to say.
You really don't know what you're
talking about."

Q. O.   "So What?"

Silence, 2 minutes.

T. Z.   "Well, what else is new?"

The group recorder strives to get word-for-word quotes from
each speaker, unless the speaker repeats herself; then the group
recorder may enter something like,

H.G.   "That's a rotten . . ." (repeats
last speech).

It is suggested that novice recorders err on the side of
recording everything they can, until an instructor or group process supervisor can review the recording and suggest observations
that could be omitted. In general, all verbal and nonverbal interactions are relevant for understanding the ebb and flow of group
interaction.

Analysis of Events

The Analysis of Events column should include all hunches about what an event seemed to mean. Not all events will have a clear meaning. However, when events are coupled, appear repeatedly, or appear to affect group interaction, guesses about their meaning can be made. For example, when each of a series of speeches by a group member is followed by a sudden, tense silence, the leader could hypothesize that the group atmosphere is changing (from cohesive to tense, or from informal to formal) in relation to that group member's behavior. Such hunches are useful because they give the nurse leader ideas about when and how to intervene in group interaction and when to remain silent.

However, since they are only hunches about the meaning of events, question marks can be placed before the analyses that require more supporting data. Examples of comments that might be placed in the Analysis of Events column are the following:

ANALYSIS OF EVENTS

anxiety increasing
rationalization
helplessness
intellectualization
dependency on leader
? pairing
? scapegoating
expected orientation behavior
? group moving into working phase
decision reached by consensus
unilateral decision
? group norm of politeness
? competition for leadership
? competition for leader approval
? theme: "We're deprived"

? theme: "We're different"
informal leader behavior—
     summarizing
informal leader behavior—
     giving feedback
informal leader behavior—
     clarifying
unclear—uses indefinite pronouns

Leader Action

The Leader Action column should include all verbal and non-verbal communications of the designated leader of the group. This column, then, together with column 1 (Events) should contain all the verbal and nonverbal interaction of the session. When written records are being kept, columns 1 and 3 are filled in during the group session. Columns 2, 4, and 5 are filled in after the group session is over.

Evaluation of Leader Action

Suggestions for comments that might be placed in this column indicate effective or ineffective action.

EVALUATION OF LEADER ACTION

effective—tension decreased
ineffective—? countertransference toward H. G.
effective—Q. R. started verbalizing feelings
ineffective—asked two questions at once
ineffective—asked a "yes/no" question
effective—redefined goals

effective—placed responsibility with
the group
ineffective—insufficient introduction
ineffective—apathy continues
effective—decision reached by
consensus
ineffective—conflict
ineffective—anxious silence followed
effective—cohesiveness increased
ineffective—uneven balance between
task and maintenance functions
ineffective—nurse uses unclear
pronouns

Alternative Actions

Suggestions for more effective leader behavior are placed in the Alternative Actions column. The purpose of this column is to provide a means of suggesting more concise, clear, and effective ways of intervening.

Some alternative action comments may be more concise restatements of what was said during the session. Others may be to remain silent or to provide needed actions, such as giving responsibility to the group, validating, pointing out time limits, providing support, giving feedback, keeping the group on its task, giving information, testing for consensus, summarizing, exploring, starting the group, and keeping on the topic. Examples of each of these suggestions, in the order listed here, are given below:

ALTERNATIVE ACTIONS

Remain silent
"Several group members seemed concerned about..." (to the group)
"What's going on between Betty
and Bob?"

"If I understand you right, you have
        mixed feelings about surgery."
"We have 10 minutes left to talk
        today."
"I guess I would feel upset, too."
"That sounds reasonable."
"Let's move on to discuss day care
        now."
"I'm Jan Shawn, a nurse. I'll be lead-
        ing this group today."
"Are we all agreed then?"
"Today we covered how gastritis
        occurs and what different people
        do to decrease it."
"Say more about that"
"Let's all introduce ourselves"
"We're off the track; we were discus-
        sing birth control."

Figure 9 shows a sample recording for a group of children who
have diabetes. Notice the location of comments in each column
of the recording. The interactions can be numbered to enable
the reader to follow the comments in the sequence in which they
were made.

Figure 9

Sample Recording of Group Interaction for Children with Diabetes

Events	Leader Analysis	Leader Action	Evaluation	Alternative Action
M shakes head No	?Anxiety; expected behavior when a new member enters the group	"Would you like to introduce yourself, M?"	Not a good question because it can be answered with yes or no	"This is M, a new group member."
P has parka over head, body turned away from M		"Perhaps E and K could help me tell the new member what we have discussed so far."	Shares responsibility with the group	Leader could review; could ask members how they "feel about having a new member"
E, "I forgot."				
K, "There's a new injector for insulin. You pull the trigger."		"Uh huh, in a few minutes we'll get K to show us the gun."	Half-heartedly acknowledges K's remembrance of the last session	"Yes, that's right; show us the injector."
3-minute silence with group members moving in chairs	Anxious silence	"I know we talked about food last week. What kind of diet is everyone on?"	Perhaps leader is anxious about how to deal with new member and so breaks the silence	
H, "What time is this over?"	Anxious; wish to get away from uncomfortable situation	"The group is over in half an hour."	Task function of giving information	

USING RECORDINGS

Recording group interaction is a tedious but rewarding task. Students often complain about the time and effort involved, but they also always comment on the helpfulness of recordings in learning group skills.

Recordings can be used in a number of ways. They can provide the learner with information about what happened in the group, what to observe in the future, and what would have been more effective leader action. Novice group leaders are often so busy participating in the group that they do not absorb these events and interactions unless recordings are made.

Recordings are often shared with a supervisor or instructor who can use the information about a leader's group skills to provide feedback. When this is to be done, space is left for supervisory comments to be inserted between events recorded.

Another use of recordings is to provide information to use in assessing the leader's progress in developing group skills. Figure 10 shows a group skills checklist that can be used to evaluate leadership skills.

Some instructors or supervisors may prefer that the learner abstract recording difficulties and group problems that need to be solved. Figure 11 shows a report sheet that group members can use to abstract information from the complete group recording.

Still another way for the nurse group leader to gain group skills is to present group interaction recordings orally to an instructor and/or to a group of other nurses who are learning about group process. Entire recordings may be presented if time permits. If only 30 to 45 minutes are allowed for a presentation, the student can use the brief presentation form for group interaction, as shown in Figure 12.

Figure 10
Group Skills Checklist

Orientation Phase

1. ____ Completes introductions
2. ____ States purpose of group
3. ____ Starts group action/keeps it moving
4. ____ Brings information to the group
5. ____ Gives feedback
6. ____ Clarifies
7. ____ Summarizes events
8. ____ Helps group focus on task
9. ____ Encourages clear, direct
        communication between members
10. ____ Diagnoses apathy and intervenes
11. ____ Diagnoses monopolizing and intervenes
12. ____ Diagnoses conflict and intervenes
13. ____ Diagnoses scapegoating and intervenes
14. ____ Places responsibility for decisions with group
15. ____ Identifies group norms
16. ____ Encourages ventilation of feelings
17. ____ Relieves tension
18. ____ Voices group feeling
19. ____ Identifies themes

Working Phase

1. ____ Encourages description of problems or goals
2. ____ Encourages statement of alternate actions
3. ____ Allows group to do most of talking
4. ____ Helps group evaluate their decisions
5. ____ Tests for group consensus
6. ____ Identifies transferences and countertransferences

Termination Phase

1. ____ States length of group experience
2. ____ Reminds members that group experience will end in 2 sessions
3. ____ Assists group to discuss thoughts and feelings about the group ending
4. ____ Uses last group to summarize and evaluate group experience

Figure 11
Group Problems Report Sheet

Recording difficulties:

Group problems:

Describe specific examples of problems you found in the group you observed.

Consider these problems in terms of the following behaviors:

anxiety

conflict

apathy

decision making

task leadership

maintenance leadership

monopolizing

scapegoating

pairing

cohesiveness

silences

dependency

disruptions

competition

themes

transferences/countertransferences

Figure 12
Brief Presentation Form for Group Interaction

Divide your presentation of the following topics into four time segments:

1. Problems encountered with this group.

2. Themes (give one or two examples of each theme).

3. Transferences and countertransferences.

4. Problems for which you need help in solving.

SAMPLE RECORDINGS AND EVALUATIONS

Condensed examples of a session of a task group, a teaching group, and a supportive group follow. Each recording is evaluated in terms of leadership skills, and suggested interventions are offered.

A Task Group Recording

Figure 13 presents the recording of a task group session.

Assessment of Group Leader's Effectiveness

The atmosphere of the group from beginning to end is one of casual communication; it is almost gossipy. This is not unexpected, since the participants have been classmates for two years. Perhaps because of relationships with her peers, the leader has difficulty establishing her leadership position in the group. Her very first comment indicates that she will give the group responsibility for making decisions. Unfortunately, there is no decision that is open to choice by the group, since the purpose of the group has already been established.

The casual atmosphere continues as members arrive late and share lunches. The leader makes no acknowledgment of the latecoming member. Some pairing occurs as members 7 and 9 develop a subgroup interaction. Next, the leader does take charge of the group, but she does so in an ineffective fashion. By making a unilateral decision about when decisions are to be reached and by suggesting how to proceed, she does not encourage the group to decide on how to plan its course. Perhaps as a reaction to this, member 3 states opposition to the leader's idea. At this point, member 5 shows her anxiety and unsureness by questioning the recording procedure. The leader attempts to explore this query somewhat but does not clarify the group contract or elicit the member's concerns about recording. Next, tension is partially relieved by laughter and somewhat defused by returning to a topic that does not require members to take a stand against the leader and risk rejection.

The leader seems to benefit from the decrease in tension and is able to acknowledge a group member's suggestion; by doing so, she rewards making suggestions and promotes decision making and shared leadership. Group cohesiveness increases as member 4 joins in the task. At this point, the pairing activity of members 9 and 8 begins to interfere more seriously with group movement toward the goal. Member 7 asserts a leadership function and refocuses the group to its task. This action appears to increase cohesiveness again. The leader encourages movement toward the goal by rewarding and accepting suggestions. She does not seem to notice that member 2 has not participated actively in the group, and at this point, perhaps due to noninvolvement, that person leaves the group. The leader then switches from pursuit of the group goal to an unrelated topic. The group takes its cue from the leader, and from this point on the group makes no movement toward its goal.

Leadership skills during this task group session can be assessed to some extent. The leader seems able to tolerate anxiety within the group, but the levels were never very high. She is hesitant about establishing herself as leader, which may be due to her unsureness and to unrealistic expectations about what her role entails; in such a situation a novice leader can become quite anxious, and consequently her leadership skills will diminish. She does not exhibit any overt hostility or confronting behavior. The only incident that might lead to a confrontation occurs when number 3 says "Oh, no" in response to the leader's suggestion. Since neither person pursues the disagreement, no hostility develops.

Since it is not possible to know her inner thoughts, the only way to evaluate how well the leader organizes and understands group process is to observe how she responds to the process. One clue here is the leader's response to member 5, who questions the recording procedure. By responding to this comment, the leader shows that she recognizes anxiety in the group.

Figure 13
Recording of a Task Group Session

Seating Arrangement

```
7   8   9         4 = leader
6       1         1 = recorder
    2
5   4   3
```

Date: 2/27/77

Group: 2nd meeting
Planning Committee for Class Follies

Events	Leader Analysis	Leader Action	Evaluation	Alternative Action
7 "A skit could be made out of bedmaking."	7 Is involved and comfortable	4 "Do you want to talk about the Follies?"		Should not have given a choice
9 arrives late; shares lunch with 8	? Pairing	4 "Today we're going to make definite decisions about what to include."		
		4 "I thought we could use popular songs and have themes."	Task function of stating purpose	
3 "Oh, no."		4 "Yes, is that O.K.?"		
5 "Is 1 recording this?"	Group takes pressure off leader by returning to previous subject			Leader could have reassured group that discussion was confidential
Group laughs				
5 "We could impersonate faculty."		4 "Good idea. Some of you can do that."	Acknowledges suggestion and expands on it; part of decision-making process	

4 "7 does; she imitates R real well!"	4 Becomes more active and makes first verbal comment			
9 "I acted out a real vignette at work the other night."	9 and 8 pair off			
8 "What happened?"				
7 "I'd like to do something like Truth is Stranger than Fiction"	Leadership function refocuses group to its task			
9 "Oh, yes."				
8 "We could do our VW skit!"	?Cohesiveness increases	4 "Those all sound good. Let's have them one at a time."	Maintenance function of accepting task function of suggesting	
6 "What about . . . ?"				
2 "I have to leave; see ya."				Might have asked 2 to stay
8 "I thought of another one; well, that's irrelevant."		4 "Go ahead and tell us."	Leader responds to 8's enthusiasm	Refocus
8 relates work incident		4 "Don't you wonder if that will happen to you?"	joins unrelated topic	
9 "It did." Group continues to discuss work incidents		4 "We'll have to end soon."	Task function of giving information	

In her analysis, the leader also notes when member 4 begins to participate verbally in the group. When member 9 begins to discuss irrelevant work incidents, it is not clear whether the leader remains silent because she wants the group to take responsibility for refocusing, or because she is unaware of the process that is occurring. Since this is only the second session of the group, it is unlikely that the leader has already taught group members to assume responsibility for leadership functions. It is possible, however, that member 7 has developed refocusing skills through other group experiences. When the leader herself joins in topics unrelated to the group purpose, it becomes clear that she does not completely understand the group process that is occurring.

The leader does seem to have spent some time thinking about the group goal and is probably aware of its importance to group process. This is evident from her third comment, when she suggests a direction the group might take in working toward the goal.

The leader does not ask the group to assist with group functions, or record that the supervisor's assistance is requested. However, merely by using the process recording method, she clarifies areas in which assistance is needed; and by giving the record to a supervisor or instructor, feedback can be obtained.

There are no examples of the leader's use of humor in the recording. Although the group members laugh at one point, this seems to be anxious laughter used to release tension.

The leader shows several signs of prompting independence in group members. For example, she allows them to take leadership in refocusing the discussion. Also, she promotes independence by telling them that they can share in developing skits to impersonate faculty members and that they can help to develop skit ideas one by one.

The leader seems to have mixed feelings about being a leader with her peers. She is able to fulfill partially the task-leader functions of getting the group going, stating the group purpose, acknowledging and promoting exploration of suggestions, and giving information. Some task functions that she does not fulfill (or encourage others to fulfill) include clarifying the group task, keeping the group moving toward its goal, clarifying unclear statements, pointing out movement toward or away from the goal, restating, and teaching the group to solve problems.

The leader partially fulfills the maintenance function of acceptance by telling group members that they make good suggestions. One of the maintenance functions the leader does not fulfill (or encourage others to fulfill) is to give support to anxious or unsure members. For example, member 5 seems anxious about the recording procedure, and member 2 may have left due to anxiety. Other functions left unfilled are relieving tension, promoting attraction for the group, voicing group feeling, and helping the group to evaluate itself. This is not completely unexpected, since task group leaders often focus more intensively on the group goal and tend to ignore maintenance functions.

In the condensed group recording, the leader does not use the communication techniques of paraphrasing, behavior description, feeling description, or validating. Perhaps because the leader is so involved in the group task and work incidents, she focuses more on stating the purpose, decision making, and giving information.

The leader records no reactions to group processes. This is probably understandable in the beginning leader, who is preoccupied with directing the group and ensuring that the mechanical aspects of group structure are fulfilled. However, as a leader progresses in the development of leadership skills, it is expected that she will begin to be more aware of her thoughts and feelings about what happens in the group, and of how she responds to group members' attempts to cast her in a role or to evoke under- or overreactions.

How could the leader intervene to make this task group session more constructive and fruitful? An assessment of leadership skills can serve as a guide to the supervisor or instructor in suggesting possible interventions to the nurse group leader. Some of the functions the leader of this group did not fulfill have already been discussed.

One suggested intervention in this instance might be for the leader to provide a clearer statement of the group goal or purpose. For example, the leader needs to be more specific about decisions the group is to make during that session. She could state, "We're here to agree on five skits to include in the Class Follies." Another way to clarify the group goal would be to ascertain group members' reactions to the stated goal by asking outright, "What are your feelings about completing that task today?"

In these examples and in the interventions that follow, the leadership function could be provided by the designated leader or by one of the other group members. The leader might ask a group member to state (or restate) the group purpose, and to ask for feedback, or a group member might volunteer to state the group purpose and to test for group reactions. In some groups, the designated leader may not be the most skilled of the members in assuming group functions and/or may not have taught others how to assume group functions.

Although the leader notes that member 5 is concerned about the recording, no specific alternative action is suggested. One that could be used is, "This information on the recording is shared only with my supervisor for learning purposes. How do you feel about having this meeting recorded?"

The next significant event not dealt with by the leader is the leave-taking of number 2. If this person's silence is observed early in the session, the leader might try to draw the silent member into the group by saying, "What are you thinking about?" or "What is your reaction to this discussion?" Even if the leader does miss the silent member's clues, she might say when the member is about to leave, "Leaving?" or "We only have 15 minutes left today, and we really need your input." Sometimes just by questioning the leave-taking, or by reinforcing the members' commitment to the group, the leader can promote attraction for the group and the common good.

Another event that requires the leader's intervention is the switch in group focus from the group goal to work incidents. In this case, the leader might comment, "We're off the track," or "Tell us after the meeting," or "let's get back to the skits for the Follies."

Some of the missing leader functions may be the result of inexperience in acting as group leader. Others may be due to the leader's inability to cope with her own mixed feelings about being leader in a group of her peers. Thus, a suggested preventive intervention would be for the leader to examine her reactions to members. Although it is often useful to be liked by group members, this is not always a prerequisite to the leader's helpfulness to a group. If the need to be accepted, liked, and approved by group members exceeds or equals the wish to be helpful, the leader's need may successfully interfere with effective leading of the group. For these reasons, leaders would be well advised to seek out supervision from a more experienced group leader until they have gained considerable experience.

Assessment of Group Recorder's Skills

The group recorder has reported seating arrangement, date of the meeting, the names of the leader and the recorder, and the purpose of the group. Events and leader actions are clearly stated. Quotation marks are used to separate verbal statements from nonverbal communications. The Analysis of Events column contains no observed behaviors; analyses that have little data to support them are preceded by question marks.

This recording could be improved by making two changes. First, observations regarding lack of leader reactions to the group should have been placed in the fourth column. Examples of comments that could have been included in that column are, "Vying with group member for leadership," "Angry with group member," and "Anxious about beginning the group."

Second, specific statements or behaviors are called for in the fifth column. Instead, the suggestions found there are general in nature. Specific alternative actions that might be suggested are, "Let's talk about the Follies," "The recordings will be shared only with my supervisor," "Leaving?" and "Tell us after the meeting is over."

Figure 14

Recording of a Teaching Group Session for Expectant Mothers

Seating Arrangement

N = leader
M = recorder

```
D        A
     J
   N   M
```

Date: 4/14/77

Group: *Prenatal Teaching Group*

Events	Leader Analysis	Leader Action	Evaluation	Alternative Action
			No introduction of new group leader	"I'm the new leader for today."
A giggles	Anxiety	"Do you know what to expect when labor begins?"	A yes/no question	"Who can tell us the signs of labor beginning?"
		"There are several signs; one is the bloody show, another is the breaking of waters."		
A "I was wondering because I dribble when I sneeze; is that urine or water?"	A voices a potential source of anxiety	"It was probably not the waters; have you felt crampy?"	Clarifies; seeks information	"Anyone in the group have an answer?" or "Urine is yellow; if you wear a Kotex you can tell."
		"Those are probably the Braxton Hicks contractions we talked about."	Clarifying; seeking information; giving information	
A "I read about those."	?Seeking leader approval	Refers to course outline	Some anxiety; retreats to paper	"Perhaps you could tell the group what you read."

A "Yesterday I felt the baby pushing. It scared me."	Theme: anxiety about delivery	"If you feel nervous, sit down and relax."	Gives solution for A's fear. Could have explored this further	"What scared you?" or "Being scared is a natural reaction" or "Have others felt scared?"
Members lie on floor and practice muscle control and breathing exercises		"Do you want to practice Kegel exercises?"	A yes/no question	"Let's practice Kegel exercises; they prevent dripping urine"
		Leader coaches and gives each feedback on how each has mastered the exercise	A delayed response, but effective in reinforcing and evaluating learner's exercise abilities	
J enters and exercising stops	Disruption by member who comes late		Leader does not acknowledge entrance	"J's here. She usually leads the group. Do you want to take over now, J?"
Group resumes exercises J starts coaching them			?Conflict and/or competition	
		"That's right, D."	Vying for leadership but does not settle how to work together directly	
Members turn first to J and then to N for help J "The students can help you."	Group unclear about who is leader	"Do you want this seat, J?"	N defers leadership to J without discussing it; could use this situation to teach shared leadership	"I'll help with the exercises. Do you want to do the talking, J?"
	J differentiates leader from students			

A Teaching Group Recording

Figure 14 presents the recording of an early session of a teaching group. The focus of the group is on teaching pregnant women about physiological, anatomical, and emotional changes that occur during pregnancy, and on physical exercises that are useful during pregnancy, labor, and delivery.

Assessment of Group Leader's Effectiveness

From the beginning of the session, there is no casualness or socializing in this group. The leader gets right down to business and even omits important orienting information. The atmosphere of the session is formal as the nurse teacher starts by imparting information and the group members by asking for information. Not unexpectedly, themes of anxiety and conflict are noticeable in this early group session.

Member A is the most verbal group member. Although her talkativeness creates no problems at this point, it is a signal to the leader to watch for the process of monopolizing. Member A's behavior may also be viewed as that of group spokesman; anxiety is not an unusual reaction to anticipated delivery, and member A may be voicing a fear that others in the group share.

The group continues, and the previous leader arrives unexpectedly while they are practicing breathing exercises. At this point a disruption occurs, as the leader's focus of attention shifts from the group to working out a coleading relationship. Because neither the leader nor the ex-leader deals with this issue directly, most of the rest of the session is used to work it out indirectly.

Leadership skills during the teaching group session can be assessed to some extent. The leader seems to have an adequate tolerance for anxiety. In addition, she is able to observe, identify, and focus on expressed anxiety. Labeling the member's feeling as "nervousness" gives the leader an opening to suggest possible interventions, such as sitting down and practicing exercises when anxious.

There are no evidences of hostility among group members. If anything, extreme dependency and compliance are demonstrated as the members turn continually to the leader for advice and assistance. The leader, in turn, demonstrates her dependency on J by deferring to her as if she were the authority, rather than giving her feedback about how to work together. J accepts the authoritarian role, thus passing up a chance to show the group how to establish a collaborative relationship by discussing this situation in the group.

By identifying and intervening in anxiety, the leader demonstrates an understanding of that group process. She also seems to recognize symptoms of dependency when she speculates that member A may be seeking leader approval. Whether the leader understands the process of what occurs between herself and the previous leader at the time that this is happening is less clear. There are additional written notes speculating on how this disruption is affecting both the group and the designated leader. It may be that the leader (or recorder) only understands the conflict/competition process after reviewing the written record of the session. Nevertheless, both observations are astute and lead to useful alternative actions after the fact, if not to actual interventions at the time the event occurred.

There is only indirect evidence that the leader made any preparations for leading the group. She seemed prepared in terms of teaching content and of trying to use and apply group process theory to group events, but apparently she had not thought much about or was unable to implement a smooth beginning for the session.

In her first comment, the leader asks the group to assist with group functions by asking them for information. Most of the rest of her comments seem to be attempts to provide leadership functions herself, except when she defers to J, the ex-leader.

Neither the leader nor the group recorder requests assistance. However, merely recording and turning in a written record is one way of asking for assistance from a more experienced group leader. There are no examples of humor in this recording. On the contrary, an atmosphere of seriousness prevails.

The leader makes no attempt to promote independence in

group members. One wonders whether she is aware that she may be promoting member A's dependent bids for attention by not encouraging group members to take more responsibility for group functioning.

The leader seems to move easily into the traditional teaching role. Most of her statements are of an information-giving or -gathering nature. The leader fulfills the task functions of getting the group going and clarifying unclear statements. Some task functions she does not fulfill are stating the group purpose, acknowledging and exploring group members' suggestions, keeping the group moving toward its goal, pointing out movement toward or away from the group goal, restating, and teaching the group to solve problems.

The leader fulfills the maintenance functions of accepting (by telling D she was doing an exercise correctly) and of giving support (by suggesting a solution for member A's anxiety). She may be trying to relieve high tension levels in the group by suggesting a release through physical exercise. Some maintenance functions the leader does not fill are voicing group feeling, promoting attraction for the group, and helping the group to evaluate itself. Unlike the leader in the foregoing task group recording, this leader does make an attempt to balance task functions with maintenance functions.

The leader does not use paraphrasing, behavior description, feeling description, or validating. She does use feedback by telling member D that she is doing an exercise correctly.

A specific communication problem is demonstrated by the use of yes/no questions. Since the leader's role involves facilitating communication, it is important for her to speak as little as possible and to allow others to speak more frequently. When the leader uses yes/no questions, the group members answer with a brief yes or no.

In the beginning of the session, the leader has a tendency to give information rather than to find out what group members already know and what they could teach one another. Then, when the previous leader enters, the present leader directs observation and communication primarily toward her, but in an indirect manner. Thus, neither serves as a role model by teaching the group how to work out a collaborative relationship, nor do they concentrate on being effective communicators with group members.

The leader recorded several of her own reactions to group events. First, she notes her anxiety when perceiving a challenge to give information about Braxton Hicks contractions. Perhaps because she feels unsure about her knowledge in this area, she retreats to her course outline to decrease her anxiety. Second, the leader recognizes the delay between A's expressed concern about losing urine and the leader's suggestion that the group practice Kegel exercises. Third, after the group session, the leader identifies her feelings of conflict about competition with the other leader.

What interventions could be made to improve group functioning? First of all, the leader of this formal, serious group could well consider introducing some fun, lightness, and relaxation into the situation. By using warming-up exercises along with humor, the leader could give the group atmosphere a much happier tone. Also, if the leader feels comfortable doing so, she could share her own thoughts and feelings as a way of increasing cohesiveness and decreasing formality.

Independence in group members could be promoted by asking them to share information with one another, to turn to one another—rather than the leader—for assistance, and to participate in problem-solving efforts. This will require the leader to step out of the role of "expert" and share leadership functions with the group, a difficult thing for the novice group leader to do when she is struggling to learn the basic mechanics of directing a group. It might be helpful for her to comment, "Who has an answer for that?" or "Tell us what you read." Both statements will increase independent action by prompting group members to provide information.

Some maintenance functions could be filled by the leader making such comments as, "I wonder if others in the group are worried about dribbling urine?" or "I wonder what feelings others have about delivery?" or "I'm not sure what to do here, J; I'm not sure how we should work out our relationship as leaders."

In the task function area the leader could state the group purpose more clearly at the beginning of the session. She might say, "This is the third meeting of the prenatal teaching group. Tonight we will focus on your concerns about delivery," or "This is our third meeting. Our focus tonight is anticipated labor problems, and how you plan to deal with them." Because the leader is unclear about the focus of her teaching, the content shifts from labor to problems of pregnancy to delivery to exercise practice. Although a leader must be flexible enough to respond to emerging group needs, it is always helpful to plan what will be covered during that teaching session. If the leader has a plan and refocuses on the issues at hand, the anxious member's potentially monopolizing behavior can be reduced. She can also direct the discussion to the topic of the meeting by asking others for their reactions about that topic. With the session proceeding as it is, only member A is able to verbalize her feelings. By trying to link others' responses to member A's statements, a discussion rather than a dialogue may ensue. Sample statements that may be beneficial in reversing the dialogue situation are, "Who else has an idea about that?" or "What's your reaction to what A said?"

The leader shows unsureness about how to proceed by asking the group to decide how to begin and structure the group. Also, the way she words her questions demonstrates some weakness in communication skills. It is possible to structure group events and get feedback from the group at the same time. For example, the leader could say, "Let's begin talking about labor. What thoughts do you have about what to expect?" or, "We could practice the exercise right now that decreases urine dribbling; what's your reaction to this idea?" Neither of these questions can be answered with a simple yes or no, and thus they encourage the group to share ideas and participate in decision making.

Assessment of Group Recorder's Skills

The initial information about seating arrangement, date, and so on seems to be appropriate. Events and leader actions are clearly recorded. Verbal communication has been placed in quotation marks to differentiate it from nonverbal communication. The analysis of events contains proper information since only the leader's ideas about what occurred are recorded there.

The record shows that the leader and/or group recorder have spent time thinking about and evaluating their feelings about group events. The ability to observe oneself objectively is a group skill of high order. Specific statements are recorded in the Alternative Action column. In general, this recording demonstrates a high level of skill.

A Supportive Group Recording

Figure 15 represents the recording of a supportive group or "rap session" for adolescents who have diabetes. The focus of the group is on sharing interpersonal situations and knowledge related to the diabetic experience.

Assessment of Group Leader's Effectiveness

Of the three sample recordings that have been presented, this one reveals the highest level of self-disclosure. Perhaps this finding is not completely unexpected, since supportive groups zero in on personal thoughts and feelings. However, the leader also demonstrates a level of communication skill and ease that the other two leaders did not.

The leader discharges her responsibility by reviewing the group contract and encouraging all group members to participate by sharing in introductions. Member dependency and low self-disclosure occurs when they initially look to the leader and deny difficulties with diabetes. When the leader assists group process by pointing to how similar they are in their reactions to diabetes, the potential for group cohesiveness increases, and there is greater freedom to discuss difficulties. Tension is further released through group laughter, which may be laughter of recognition; group members may have shared the experiences of being treated differently because of their diabetes.

Figure 15

Recording of a Supportive Group for Adolescents with Diabetes

Seating Arrangement

7 = recorder
8 = leader

```
   3  4  5
 2         6
   1  8  7
```

Date: 3/15/77

Group: Rap Session for Adolescents with Diabetes

Events	Leader Analysis	Leader Action	Evaluation	Alternative Action
All members look at leader		Reviews group contract Leans forward on chair with hands partially covering face	Task function of getting group going Mixed message via body language	Remove hands from face
Members state their names but look at leader while doing so; all deny difficulties with diabetes	Dependency and low-level self-disclosure characteristic of orientation phase	"Let's go around the group introducing ourselves."	Leader could encourage more disclosure	"What else would you like us to know about you?"
6 "I had a teacher once who acted like I had a contagious disease." Group laughs	6 Decreases group tension	"I think it's interesting that no one's been hampered by diabetes."	Tries to increase cohesiveness by pointing out similarity	"No problems at all because you have diabetes?"
			Could introduce doubt to decrease denial	
3 "I try to keep it a secret from teachers."		"How did you feel then?"	Leader tries to explore feeling	"Have others had a similar reaction?"

Member behavior	Commentary	Leader response	Commentary	Alternative response
4 "Most of my friends know. There's one teacher who refers to it as my problem."	?Group compares leader with other authority figures	"Sounds like some teachers could use some health teaching themselves."	Supports 3, but may be over-protective due to irritation with teachers	"How come?"
3 Proceeds with long monologue with theme of being misunderstood especially about diet	Potential monopolizing member; may be seeking approval or recognition		Need to try to relate 3's difficulties to others'	"Anyone else feel as 3 does?" or "What does the group think about what 3 is saying?"
2 "I always have food hidden in my room."	Level of self-disclosure deepens with sharing of a secret			
6 and 4 "Me too!"	Cohesiveness increasing in most of group members	"You have something in common." Goes on to discuss why diet is important	Promotes cohesiveness then tries to retain leadership by redirecting the focus; is leader anxious here?	Silence
General discussion about sneaking food				
3 Looks at leader and does not join in	May be testing to see if leader will respond as mother does	"Do you resent that?"	Labels feeling without validating it	"What's your reaction to that?"
6 "No matter what's wrong, my mother says it's due to diabetes." Looks at leader				
5 "I always know when I'm going to have a reaction."	First time 5 spoke 3 and 1 are potential isolates in this group	"Let's talk a little about reactions."	Seeks to explore a topic	
All but 3 and 1 join in a discussion of reactions		"Time's up for today. See you next week."	Takes responsibility for ending group	"Let's summarize what happened today."

It is not unusual for group members to perceive the group leader as a teacher. For this reason it is possible that the discussion about teachers may be an attempt to compare and contrast the leader's responses to other authority figures' behavior. Some thoughts group members may be having in this area are: Will this person be like other adults I know? Will I be understood here? Can I be safe and comfortable here so I can share my thoughts and feelings? Instead of recognizing this process, the leader sides with the students and makes a slightly derogatory comment about the teacher.

The leader shows some irritation, and a monologue concerning being misunderstood follows. It could be that the members feel that the leader misinterpreted their earlier testing behavior of comparing authority figures, and so member 3 speaks for the group and tells about feeling misunderstood. Also member 3's behavior may be seen as monopolizing. The leader seems not to recognize or at least not to know how to deal with monopolizing as it occurs. Perhaps the leader's silence was helpful because members 2, 4, and 6 feel secure enough to share a secret. With this increase in self-disclosure, group cohesiveness increases. At the same time, member 3 continues to try to have a special relationship with the leader, as exemplified by the fact that she does not join in the secret-sharing activity and looks toward the leader instead.

Perhaps the leader becomes anxious with the level of self-disclosure shown, because no sooner has she increased cohesiveness and sharing than she increases distance in the group by taking the teacher role of information-giver. Member 6 continues testing to see if the leader is like other authority figures—in this case, his mother. The leader tries to explore the member's relationship with his mother, but she puts some words into his mouth by labeling his feeling as resentment rather than by allowing him to describe his own feeling.

Despite the leader's action, member 5, who has been silent until now, is able to assert herself as an independent person who knows as well as her mother when she is going to have a hypo- or hyperglycemic reaction. It is interesting that member 5 chooses this point at which to speak. It may be that this person has been observing the others' behavior, including the leader's, and only now feels comfortable enough to join in. Or number 6's comment may be one that number 5 can identify with. The leader makes a judgment at this time that the topic of reactions has relevance for the whole group and so tries to explore it further. In the process of this group, as in all groups, a number of events occur during the session that make it necessary for the leader to decide when and how to intervene. Part of this decision-making process is based on theory and timing; part of it is related to the leader's personal style and experience in handling various group events.

As the session ends, the leader introduces more structure into the group by calling attention to the end of the meeting. She also encourages its ongoing quality by stating her intention to see the members at the next session.

There are three times during this meeting when the leader's anxiety has potential for influencing group process. The first occurs at the beginning of the session, when the leader gives a mixed communication message. The verbal message is "I am open and interested," while the nonverbal message is "I am closed off and distant." It is quite likely that this mixed message is caused by the leader's anxiety. If the leader's ability to tolerate anxiety were evaluated on the basis of this message alone, the conclusion would be that the leader might have shown more tolerance for anxiety had she not given a mixed message and had she been able consciously to remove her hands from her face.

The second occurrence of anxiety is less clear. It is probable that the leader experiences some anxiety when member 6 brings up the example of being mistreated by a teacher who "acted like I had a contagious disease." The leader's anxiety then may be due to her unmet, but unrealistic expectations of teachers, to the member's attempt to evoke a sympathetic response from the leader, or to some other reaction. Despite the cause, it is fairly clear that leader anxiety is converted into irritation or anger; such conversion is not unusual and is the kind that group leaders need to watch for in themselves and in other group members. If the leader had a higher tolerance for anxious feelings, she might not have to convert her discomfort into irritation or anger.

The third time the leader's anxiety is evident is when she deflects the group focus from disclosure and cohesiveness to a more neutral topic. Changing topics is a common reaction to anxiety. Again, if the leader had a greater tolerance for anxiety, she might not need to change the subject and thereby increase distance between herself and the group. Anxiety is more likely to occur in a less structured group, such as a supportive one, where guidelines for behavior are less clear and the expectations of higher levels of self-disclosure can increase discomfort. For these reasons, the leader of a supportive group needs to be especially skilled in identifying and dealing with anxiety in self and others.

There are no examples of hostility among group members; all seem to be trying to get along with one another and to impress the leader. This is expected behavior in early group sessions.

The group recorder's analyses of events and evaluation of leader action give some clues to how well the leader understands group process. There is evidence of application of group theory and of such concepts as dependency, self-disclosure, monopolizing, cohesiveness, testing, isolation, communication, and denial. The leader also demonstrates an ability to understand her own anxiety and irritation in reaction to group processes.

There is only indirect evidence that the leader had thought through how to proceed with the group session. For example, she begins the group effectively by reviewing the group contract and starting group introductions. She also has decided how to end the group. The middle part of the session seems to have been less well thought out; at one point the leader begins to teach about diabetic diets; whether this is due to insufficient preplanning or spur-of-the-moment anxiety is not clear.

The leader asks the group to share in introductions. She makes some attempt to get group members to talk to one another when she points out their similarities, but she could make more attempts to have group members ask one another questions and react to comments, rather than expecting the leader to direct and comment on what is said.

Neither the leader nor the group recorder requests any

assistance. However, producing a written record is itself one way the inexperienced leader can ask for assistance.

Although there is laughter in this group, it is unclear whether humor is intended. Here, as in the task group recording (Figure 13), laughter may be primarily tension-relieving behavior. In this case, exaggeration is a factor in the member's comments, and this could be the basis for the laughter. The leader herself makes no use of humor during the session.

The leader promotes independence by asking group members to introduce themselves and by suggesting that the group explore diabetic reactions more thoroughly. Both of these actions imply that the leader considers the group members as capable of performing these tasks.

In the Alternative Action column the leader makes further suggestions about how she could have promoted independence. She says she could have asked the group to compare and contrast their reactions ("Have others had a similar reaction?" and "Anyone else feel as 3 does?"), or to summarize what happened or what they accomplished in that group session.

When the leader remains silent, the group is forced to take responsibility for group functioning. Thus, silence can be an effective method of encouraging the group to take responsibility for keeping the group process moving. Here, the leader is able to let go partially of the directing reins. When self-disclosure becomes uncomfortable for her, she again takes firm hold.

The leader takes some or all of the responsibility for the task functions of getting the group going, stating the group purpose, giving information, acknowledging and exploring group members' suggestions, keeping the group moving toward its goal, and ending the group. She demonstrates little direction in terms of restating, summarizing, and teaching the group to solve problems.

The leader fulfills the maintenance functions of accepting, supporting, and promoting attraction for the group by pointing out similarities between group members and by exploring feelings. She does not fill the maintenance functions of voicing group feeling and helping the group to evaluate itself, but she makes some attempt to achieve a balance between task and maintenance functions.

The leader does not use the communication techniques of paraphrasing, behavioral description, or validating. Instead of validating member 6's feeling, she labels the feeling herself. Her statement about noting that no one seems hampered by having diabetes could be viewed as a feedback statement.

One of the leader's questions is of the yes/no variety. When she asks, "Do you resent that?" her wording is ineffective for two reasons. First, the question is one that can be answered with a brief yes or no. Second, the question implies a way member 6 is expected to feel; if he does not already feel that way, the leader may be suggesting how she thinks he should feel. If the group member is quite susceptible to the influence of authority figures, he may answer yes just to receive the leader's approval.

The leader has a tendency to focus on individual problems within the group setting. The result is that she not only promotes dependency on herself (since communications are structured to go between her and another group member) but also carries on a series of one-to-one relationships under the guise of dealing with the group. She may recognize this trait after the fact, because many of her Alternative Action comments suggest ways to involve group members with one another: "Have others had a similar reaction?" "Anyone else feel as 3 does?" and, "What does the group think about what 3 is saying?"

The leader notes three of her reactions to the group. First, she points out that she gave the group a mixed message. She does not identify the feeling that led to the discordant verbal/nonverbal message, but it is likely that she recognizes it as anxiety. Such leader reaction would not be unexpected in the early part of the first group session. Had the leader noted this on her recording, it would have provided even further evidence that she is knowledgeable about group process.

Second, the leader is aware of feelings of protectiveness toward member 3. Awareness of countertransference reactions is helpful; there would be even stronger evidence of the leader's grasp of her reactions if the recording had included a statement concerning need for further supervision in this area and/or intent to pay attention to future interactions of this type with member 3.

Third, the leader recognizes that she may be anxious because the group has a high level of self-disclosure. Perhaps she feels left out or is worried that she will not be able to control how much personal material will be shared. To some extent, the leader does need to balance levels of self-disclosure so that cohesiveness is increased, yet embarrassment or high anxiety does not result. If only one group member were disclosing secrets, the leader could certainly want either to encourage others to share similar experiences or to defuse the intensity of the disclosure so that other group members will not become frightened. In this case, four of the six group members are openly sharing with one another; it therefore seems that the leader's shift to the more neutral topic of diet is primarily to meet her own inclusion or control needs.

This assessment of leader skills suggests alternative methods of handling similar group situations in the future. One suggested intervention is that the leader should study and ask for ongoing supervision regarding her tendency to overprotect and control the group. In the process of doing so, the leader may be able to encourage more independence among group members by asking them to describe, identify, explore, and suggest alternative ways of dealing with interpersonal reactions to having diabetes. Some statements that illustrate this kind of leader intervention are: "How has each of you reacted when others have ... ?", "What feeling is it that you all are talking about?", "Let's have all the group members tell a little more about their experiences with...", and "What other ways could you handle that situation in the future?"

The record suggests one comment that might have made the leader more effective in helping the group to summarize the session. Other comments she might have used are: "Today we got acquainted a little bit and began to talk about how people who don't have diabetes react to those who do. We also touched on diet and diabetic reactions. I think all three of these topics are important and that we could expand on them in future sessions." Since this is the first session of the group, it may be too early to expect group members to summarize. It is suggested that the leader act as role model for the group by summarizing the first few sessions. After that, the leader might say, "Who would like to summarize what we did today?" If no one volunteers, the leader can again summarize but add, "Summarizing is an important skill; you learn it through practice, and the group is a good place to begin." This kind of statement does not imply punishment to group members who do not volunteer, but it does point out the leader's expectations and provide a guideline for group behavior in future sessions.

Although many of the alternative action comments are stated well, some could be added or expanded. For example, the leader could suggest some alternative ways to ask the group to discuss their diabetic reactions. Two examples are: "Who wants to begin talking about his reactions?" and, "Let's go around the group and share experiences in this area."

Assessment of Group Recorder's Skills

The initial information about seating arrangement, date, and so on is adequate. Events and leader actions are clearly recorded. Verbal communication has been placed in quotation marks to differentiate it from nonverbal communication. The analysis of events contains appropriate information, since only the leader's ideas about what occurred are recorded.

The amount of information in columns 2, 4, and 5 provides evidence that the leader and/or group recorder have thought about group events and leader reactions. They make an effort to separate events—or what is observed in the group—from analysis and evaluation—or what the leader/recorder thinks and feels about what happens in the group. In general, this record shows excellent recording ability.

READINGS

Bradford, Leland, Dorothy Stock, and Murray Horowitz. "How to Diagnose Group Problems," in *Management for Nurses,* edited by Sandra Stone, Marie Berger, Dorothy Elhart, Sharon Firsich, and Shelley Jordan. St. Louis: C.V. Mosby, 1976.

Brooks, Dorothy. "Teletherapy: or How to Use Videotape Feedback to Enhance Group Process," *Perspectives in Psychiatric Care* 14(1976): 83-87.

Chopra, Amarjit. "Motivation in Task-Oriented Groups," *Journal of Nursing Administration* 3(1973): 55.

Clark, Carolyn. *Recording and Evaluating Nurse-Patient Interactions: Using the Process Recording Guide.* Garden Grove, Calif.: Trainex Press, 1975.

Cooper, Signe. "Committees That Work," *Journal of Nursing Administration* 3(1973): 30.

Dodge, Calvert. "A Review of the Use of Audiovisual Equipment in Psychotherapy," *Perspectives in Psychiatric Care* 7(1969): 248-258.

Gregorie, J., and D. Swanson. "Group Sessions for the Wives of Home Hemodialysis Patients," *American Journal of Nursing* 75(1975): 633-635.

Heller, Vera. "Handicapped Patients Talk Together," in *Nursing in the 70's,* edited by Ann Roa and Mary Sherwood. New York: John Wiley, 1973.

Johnson, David, and Frank Johnson. "Leading Discussion Groups," in *Joining Together: Group Theory and Group Skills,* edited by David Johnson and Frank Johnson. Englewood Cliffs, N.J.: Prentice-Hall, 1975.

McCann, M. "Group Sessions for Families of Post-Coronary Patients," *Supervisor Nurse* 7(1976): 17-19.

Muecke, Marjorie. "Videotape Recordings: A Tool for Psychiatric Clinical Supervision," *Perspectives in Psychiatric Care* 8(1970): 200-208.

Parsall, S. "Cancer Patients Help Each Other," *American Journal of Nursing* 74(1974): 650-651.

Radtke, Maxine, and Alan Wilson. "Team Conferences that Work," *American Journal of Nursing* 73(1973): 506-508.

Salzer, Joan. "Classes to Improve Diabetic Self-Care," *American Journal of Nursing* 75(1975): 1324-1326.

Smith, E.D. "Group Conferences for Postpartum Patients," *American Journal of Nursing* 71(1971): 112-113.

Smyth, Kathleen. "Symposium on Patient Teaching," *Nursing Clinics of North America* 6(1971): 571-806.

Stephens, Barbara. "Use of Groups for Management," *First-Line Patient Care Management*. Wakefield, Mass.: Contemporary Publishing, 1976.

Stoller, Frederick. "The Use of Videotape Feedback," in *New Perspectives in Encounter Groups*, edited by Lawrence Solomon and Betty Berzon. New York: Jossey-Bass, 1972.

Wilson, L. "Listening," in *Behavioral Concepts and Nursing Intervention*, coordinated by Carolyn Carlson. Philadelphia: J.B. Lippincott, 1970.

Wittmeyer, Alma. "Teaching by Audiotape," *Nursing Outlook* 19(1971): 162-163.

Wolff, Ilse. "Acceptance," *American Journal of Nursing* 72(1972): 1412-1415.

GLOSSARY OF
SELECTED GROUP TERMS

aggressiveness   behavior that has an element of control or manipulation of the other person.

anxiety   unexplained feeling of discomfort that occurs when expectations are not met.

apathy   a withdrawal response that can be used to cover tension and discomfort.

assertiveness   setting goals, acting on those goals in a clear and consistent way, and taking responsibility for the consequences of those actions.

behavioral modification   an approach to change that focuses on principles of learning, such as reinforcement, that can decrease unsatisfying or disruptive behavior and on increasing satisfying, goal-directed behavior.

behavior description   a statement of what was observed, without including a comment on the meaning or motive for the behavior.

closed group   a group to which new members are not added when others leave.

cohesiveness   the measure of attraction of the group for its members.

countertransference   leader response in an over- or underreactive way to group members because they evoke remembrances of earlier personal relationships of the leader.

covert content   the deeper, symbolic meaning of words.

feedback   letting group members know how they affect each other.

group conflict   reaction to being given an impossible task, having contradictory loyalties, jockeying for power or status, disliking others, or involving oneself in the task.

group contract   a written or verbal operating agreement between leader and group members.

group event   behavior of all group members except the designated leader.

group process   constant movement as group members seek to reduce the tension that arises when people attempt to have their individual needs met yet work to help meet group goals.

hidden agenda   individual member or leader goals that are at cross-purposes to group goals.

"I" messages   verbal communication that conveys the way the individual thinks or feels.

incompatible response   one that cannot be performed at the same time as the desired behavior.

maintenance functions   those that are directly related to improving interpersonal relationships within the group.

manipulation   attempt by group member to have his own needs met.

modeling   demonstrating desired behaviors.

monopolizing   a group problem wherein one group member agrees in some way with other group members to talk and thereby to protect them.

norm   rule for behavior in the group.

open group   a group to which new members can be added as others drop out.

orientation phase early group phase when anxiety is high, levels of self-disclosure are low, bids for the leader's attention or care are made, group goals are refined, and the leader models effective group behavior.

overt content superficial, agreed-upon meaning of words.

pairing behavior whereby group members pair off in twos to provide mutual support for one another through having subconversations; characteristic of the orientation phase.

prompting telling a person how to behave next.

reinforcers rewarding events that immediately follow a behavior and thus maintain its occurrence.

resistance phenomenon that occurs when people fear change or lack knowledge of or participation in the change.

scapegoating a group process wherein one or two members of the group are singled out and agree consciously or unconsciously to be targets for group hostility or advice.

shaping the reinforcement of successive approximations toward the desired behavior.

silence a communication that has various meanings.

supportive group a group whose main purpose is to share thoughts, feelings, and reactions to crises, health conditions, or interpersonal relationships.

task functions those that are directly related to the accomplishment of group goals.

task group a group with a main purpose of completing a task.

teaching group a group whose main purpose is to impart information.

termination phase the last phase, wherein the group focuses on evaluating and summarizing the group experience.

themes linkages and underlying consistent meaning in group interaction.

time out   removing the person from a pleasurable activity immediately, once undesirable behavior occurs.

token system   symbolic reward for desirable behavior that can be turned in at a later date for more concrete rewards.

transference   member response whereby aspects of former relationships are projected onto current figures in the group setting.

validating   checking with the other in a tentative way to see whether one's perceptions are correct.

warming-up exercises   exercises used to decrease group anxiety.

working phase   the middle phase in a group, when members know how to work together cooperatively, thoughts and feelings are shared more openly, and the leader needs to intervene less frequently to move the group along.

"You" message   aggressive verbal communication in which blame is placed on the other person.

INDEX